Praise for *Lead*

"Peri Chickering has traversed 20,000 foot peaks and major corporate boardrooms, guiding leaders across the globe through the territory of their own souls. Learn from a deeply experienced and genuine explorer what it means to venture into and master the true frontier territory of your Self."

—WILLIAM ISAACS, author of *Dialogue and the Art of Thinking Together*

"Unlike any leadership book on the market! *Leadership Flow* is a book for every stage of your career and life. I wish I had read it in my 20s, 30s, 40s and plan to continue to review it into my 60s and 70s. It is an anchor and guidepost all in one!"

—TERRI FIEZ, Vice Chancellor for Research and Innovation, University of Colorado, Boulder

"A beautifully written book for all who want to lead in ways that enhance the common good and their own wellbeing, offered up in the form of compelling personal stories, insights drawn from nature, and a wide range of wisdom traditions. Chickering's teachings will affirm and guide you as you bring your gifts to a world in need."

—PARKER J. PALMER, author of *On the Brink of Everything*, *A Hidden Wholeness*, *The Courage to Teach*, and *Let Your Life Speak*

"Powerful and illuminating. Weaving experience and insight, Peri Chickering calls us to a life of *listening*–in all the directions–and to the intelligence, creativity, and benefit inherent in our true nature."

—SARAH BUIE, Founding Convener, *Council on the Uncertain Human Future*

"All leadership today is situated in a profound moment of disruption. When you live and lead in such a context, what is the one thing you can rely on? The capacity to access your inner knowing. In this book Peri Chickering takes you on a journey to explore seven key directions of inner knowing. Essential reading for leading and flourishing in this time of transformation."

—OTTO SCHARMER, Co-founder of the Presencing Institute, author of *Theory U* and *Presencing*

Leadership Flow

Leadership Flow

The Unstoppable Power of Connection

Peri Chickering, PhD

FOREWORD BY CHRISTINE BADER,
author, *The Evolution of a Corporate Idealist:
When Girl Meets Oil*

SHE WRITES PRESS

Published 2021
Printed in the United States of America
Print ISBN: 978-1-64742-151-9
E-ISBN: 978-1-64742-152-6
Library of Congress Control Number: 2021906580

For information, address:
She Writes Press
1569 Solano Ave #546
Berkeley, CA 94707

Cover and interior design by Tabitha Lahr

She Writes Press is a division of SparkPoint Studio, LLC.

For my mother and father.
Thank you for giving me a
nature-filled childhood and
the space to find my own way.
Love and support always
present yet never demanding,
I grew up knowing I had a place
in the larger order of things.

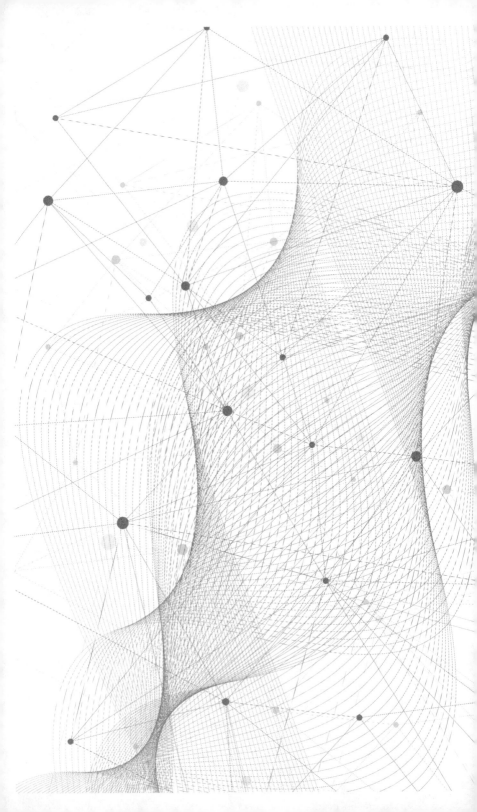

Underlying Assumption

The primary purpose of this book is to remind you of the intricate and intelligent web in which your life is embedded and to offer specific tools and practices to ensure you remain connected to this truth.

Leadership Flow is based on the fundamental assumption of an intricate and intelligent universe of which we are all a part. This assumption influences the kind of person you become and the work you are called to do. Your unique gifts and natural talents are intimately integrated into this whole. As you use these gifts, your leadership inherently flows out into the world and serves the health and well-being of all.

Awareness of this deep intelligence has been and still is being held by indigenous communities around the world. Out of respect for this longstanding wisdom, I have chosen to use an image known to Native Americans as the Seven Directions—seven domains of awareness and creative influence which work together to ensure harmony, balance, and respect for all living beings—as the central organizing structure of this book. These domains of awareness are universal, timeless, and interconnected. This book is based on my lived experience of these domains and is my own personal interpretation.

In honor of the wisdom traditions which are the foundations of this book, all proceeds from its sale will go to First Nations causes.

Contents

Foreword

*A*s the gray, damp Pacific Northwest winter arrived in late 2016, it matched my mood. The job I'd been working toward my entire career—the one I'd gone to business school for fifteen years earlier, the one I'd packed up my family and moved us across the country for, the one consuming my waking hours and mental energy—wasn't working out. But I couldn't figure out what was going wrong or what to do about it.

As I realized I needed help, one person leapt to mind. I met Peri in 2007, on a Coming into Your Own women's retreat she facilitated, and in the years since, joined two other programs for which she served as faculty.

Peri radiates assuredness and wisdom to an extent that might be intimidating or inaccessible were it not shaped by her calm stillness and infused with warmth and curiosity. When I first met her I thought, *I need more of that.*

We all do—now more than ever. As I write this in the middle of 2020, the world is in a state of breakdown: facing a global pandemic, protesting against structural racism, a looming US presidential election promising more divisiveness and chaos—all in the context of a warming planet screaming for attention.

That is why I am so thankful that Peri is finally honoring her lifelong practices in these pages for all of us to learn from.

She is not about disclosing a secret code, only available to leaders of a certain stature or privilege. Peri's superpower is reconnecting us to our true selves, to the core that has been there all along, but has been obfuscated by expectations and whatever baggage and circumstances we've accumulated on our travels.

I had lost sight of my center. Peri listened, she asked, she prodded, she played back. She breathed and reminded me to do the same. She never assumed or judged.

First, she helped me see that I didn't need to flail, that I actually was achieving much of what I had set out to achieve, that I really did have colleagues who were supporting me. With a clearer view of the landscape, Peri then guided me as I made the decision to leave my job—never imposing her own views, but asking the questions that led me to the next step.

Then, once I'd made my decision, we got tactical. Peri reminded me that not every idea has to be broadcast the moment it appears, and we thought carefully about the right sequence of whom I told and how. She schooled me in the lost art of keeping one's mouth shut, and the power and importance of being precise and deliberate when stakes are high—skills that I wish more of today's leaders had.

I left my role with more closure and gratitude than I could have ever imagined—not just given where I had been seven months earlier, but knowing how jobs usually end. I have taken a path closer to my truth, freelancing and prioritizing family and self, listening carefully for the next right move, often channeling Peri for wisdom and clarity.

Even more telling than my experience with Peri is what happened afterward. I had been gently suggesting to my husband for most of the thirteen years since we'd met that coaching might be helpful to him. But as an Englishman in finance technology on Wall Street, the notion of deep introspection out loud with another human had multiple strikes against it.

But seeing how much Peri helped me turn around my life to point in the right direction, he was moved to give her a call. They hit it off immediately, bonding over a shared love of enjoying a hot cup of tea alone atop a mountain. With completely different questions but the same steady hand, she guided him to find his way into a new creative life, which is clearly his to lead.

I've since recommended Peri to countless others, believing wholeheartedly that many people would be more effective knowing what she has to offer. To be clear: I don't mean "effective" in the sense of the productivity hacks that promise to squeeze more hours into your day and maximize your contribution to GDP. Rather, Peri has helped many people find their place in the world.

Now, because of this book, it is not only the lucky individuals who've come into personal contact with Peri that can benefit from her wisdom.

All of us deserve the connection to ourselves, our planet, and each other that Peri has long embraced and modeled and is now presenting to us. Her presence in my life has been a tremendous gift, and I know it will be for you as well.

—Christine Bader
McMinnville, Oregon
July 2020

Prologue

"We cannot live for ourselves alone. Our lives are connected by a thousand invisible threads and along these sympathetic fibers, our actions run as causes and return to us as results."

—HERMAN MELVILLE

*M*y journey in the land of leadership has been long and varied. From an early age I remember having a deep sense of confidence and self-assurance. An inner experience of "authority." Early and often, I would end up being successful in whatever was put in front of me. In school this meant I was a good student and a good athlete.

During my first year of college, rock climbing and kayaking were offered as extracurricular options. Strong and agile, I excelled in these activities, and by the following summer I had a job guiding trips for a small outdoor leadership school in Colorado. In the early 1980s it was rare to find women who not only liked spending time in the outdoors but also had some skills. My name got circulated, and soon I was leading twenty-eight-day trips for a much bigger outfit, Colorado Outward Bound School (COBS). Shouldering responsibility for the health and well-being of twelve to fifteen people for weeks on end was in essence my first formal experience of leading.

At the end of the season, I was told most of my skills were good with one exception: I needed more experience with "snow and ice." A bit of an overachiever, rather than take the readily available short courses on winter mountaineering, a couple of friends and I organized a six-week expedition to a remote and virtually uncharted mountain range in the south-central part of Alaska.

Coming Home

Dropped off in the Neacolas, I waved good-bye to our bush pilot and whispered a quiet prayer. It was mid-April and I had just turned twenty-one. My three climbing companions—Todd, Mike, and John—were equally young and inexperienced. Attempting to climb these mountains and be the first to stand on their summits, we had six weeks to listen carefully, climb with respect, and trust our pilot could remember how to find this remote and not particularly distinguishable glacier.

The team unraveled fast. On the descent of Peak Number One, Todd slipped on wet rock and went sailing off into thin air. As he zinged down the ridge line, I heard the rope running before I saw Todd's body falling. As I jammed myself into a crack in a rock, the rope went taut, catching Todd and saving us both. Mike had untied from the rope already, and I was still attached. Todd was too injured to assist himself, so we lowered him down the three thousand feet we had climbed, arriving back at our primitive base camp before daylight faded.

Seriously banged up but with no bones broken, Todd was not about to sit around for another five weeks. John had been lowered down to safety the previous night after he inadvertently kicked his gear off the tiny snow ledge where we were to rest as we waited out the darkest hours of the night. The two of them wanted out. Taking food, gear, and maps, they skied away, leaving Mike and me to fend for ourselves. Dangerous enough with four people, now down to two, we became hypervigilant, listening to any and all signals—outside or in—foreshadowing trouble. With care and specificity, going forward at times and retreating as well, we summited three peaks and made two unsuccessful attempts on Neacola Peak, the highest and only named peak in this area.

Our return to Talkeetna was scheduled for June 1. On the night of May 31, a major storm came in. For four days, the wind howled and the snow fell. With no cell phones or other means of communicating back then, my parents assumed I was dead. Four long days with no word, no sign, no Peri. Around two in the morning on day five, we were awakened by *silence*—a deep, all-pervasive quiet. As we zipped down the flap of the tent, a crystal clear and windless sky greeted us: the storm had finally ended. Grabbing our snowshoes, we marked out a landing spot as best we could in the three feet of new snow. Barely audible over the horizon came the *putt, putt, putt* of the prop plane. Intense emotions flooded my body. Relief mixed with sadness. Although ready to return to civilization, I had truly come to love these mountains and felt a deep sense of home. As the plane lifted off, I cried tears of grief. I saw Mike was crying too. I wonder now what his tears were about. I never thought to ask. Dialing my parents' number from a phone booth in Talkeetna was surreal. All my father could say when he heard my voice was "Thank God you're alive, thank God you're alive!"[1]

Three Threads

Although I didn't know it at the time, this experience in Alaska landed me squarely on one of the threads of my destiny, my connection to nature. I will tell a few stories about how the universe helped me keep a hold of this thread, which was central to both my work in the world and my experience of spirituality. Spanning the better part of two decades, the outdoors was my classroom for learning about and evoking the "inner aspects of leadership." I noticed the unique potential in the hearts and souls of each person and let the wilderness environment help bring this forward and nurture it gently into awareness. Thread number two was leadership. And thread number three surfaced through Ian, a dear friend and college buddy who climbed and kayaked with me in those early years of college. Casually and persistently, he kept mentioning this place and these people he had met. They lived nearby and perhaps I might want to check them out. Nestled in the foothills of Colorado, Sunrise Ranch was the international headquarters of a network called The Emissaries, whose expressed purpose was the "spiritual regeneration of the human race." Nonsectarian and, in those days, truly inspiring, I did, indeed, go to visit and not long afterward I moved in. I ended up at Sunrise for fourteen years.

Years of living in community with 150 others and welcoming hundreds of people from around the world was a remarkable experience of how to bring spiritual ideas into outer action. A key tenet of this network was "spirituality as practicality." Growing much of our food and hosting people on a continual basis, the phrase "before enlightenment chop wood and carry water, after enlightenment chop wood and carry water" was an apt expression for much of our outer action. Connecting the care for the land with the attitudes and emotions that arose in the midst of all these daily activities was where "inner meets outer" in this context. And this emotional and attitudinal work was taken equally seriously. Once a heated argument broke out in the group responsible for making dinner for the community, and the food was thrown out because the "energy" in which the food was prepared was one of dis-ease and disrespect.

Although Sunrise was my home base, my particular suite of skills and talents took me traveling around the world running both wilderness-based leadership programs and Art of Living courses for the community. For six months each year, I danced back and forth between community and wild places. And during this time, the three threads of my own life's work would become clear: *nature, spirituality, and leadership.* This rhythm of extensive travel also instilled an experience of "home and center" as primarily internal. I had to carry this with me wherever I went as countries, cultures, time zones, and seasons swirled around me.

My professional work gradually evolved from outside to inside. I played the role of executive director for a couple of nonprofits and was fundraiser, consultant, and trainer to start up two leadership schools. This work landed me a position as an associate professor at Regis University's Master's of Nonprofit Management program. Practicing leadership is one thing; trying to teach is a wholly different skill and one that took some time to develop competence. The seeds of this book were planted during my stint as an associate professor. Search as I might, I could not find a leadership book to use in my teaching! A plethora of books about the outer actions of leading were available but none pointing toward the inner work it takes to develop genuine authority. *Leading from Within,* a class created by a colleague and dear friend named Paul, was a beginning attempt to move thinking in this direction.

A university setting was anathema to my inherently wild nature, and I slowly began to wither in that environment. So I quit, depleted, and slowly found my way back to my sweet spot. Moving to my grandmother's home in New England, I got back to "chop wood and carry water" and began to light up again. Much to my surprise an old colleague and friend invited me to work with his small boutique consulting company, Dialogos. Migrating from a focus in the nonprofit sector, I found myself working with private sector clients and large governmental agencies, and the focus of my work became coaching and training leaders whose job was to grow other leaders.

And here I am today. In a leadership journey spanning six decades and counting, I've known the joys and dilemmas of hands-on leading, the challenges of theory building and teaching leadership, and the nuances of coaching and training leaders to grow other leaders. In all these years I have been unable to find any resource that puts in one place the suite of skills I believe are essential to lead with genuine power, authority, and intelligence. Hence, I have written this book, an "inner meets outer" kind of leadership book—grounded, practical, and embedded in a living relationship with the planet we call home. Three threads—nature, spirituality and leadership—woven together into a little book inviting you to remember your place in the larger order of things and let your leadership flow from there.

Three Spheres of Connection

In the words of Marcus Aurelius, "Meditate often on the interconnectedness and mutual interdependence of all things in the universe." Wise words for these times, the "interconnectedness and mutual interdependence of all things" is the

essential inquiry of this book. As a concept interconnectedness may not seem earth-shattering. Letting this reality be
your guide for daily living and choice making, however, may
well mean asking new questions and changing old habits.
This personal and in-depth work is the focus of *Leadership
Flow*. Designed as a roadmap for staying connected to the
larger order of things, *Leadership Flow* invites you to live at
the intersection of three spheres of connection:

○ **Your Leadership Gift:** *The unique talents that are
  yours to offer*
○ **Spirituality:** *Anchoring to the present moment,
  listening for when to act and when to stay still*
○ **Nature:** *The dynamic, interconnected, and intelligent universe in which we reside*

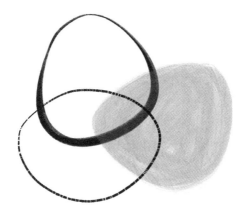

Building the muscles to stay in the sweet spot where these
three domains intersect is the purpose of this book. And it
will no doubt raise many questions. Why bother? How do
you do it? If it's so important, why isn't everyone doing it?
Does it make you more successful? More content? We will
explore these questions and many others along the way. Real
questions containing an honest blend of both skepticism

and curiosity will be your biggest guide to learning. As your questions begin to gather, let me describe the nature of the roadmap you will be using to find some answers.

Roadmap

Getting connected in the manner described in this book means embracing or at least entertaining the idea that most current ways of leading and living, intentionally or unintentionally create *separation and isolation rather than connection and community*. Finding our way back to community, to wholeness, to connection in the deepest sense of the word is key. Searching for language and images to describe this concept of wholeness has been much of my life's work. Thirty years ago, I wrote my dissertation using quantum physics to describe "A Paradigm of the Universal Whole: Toward a New Theory of Personality." My experience with a range of spiritual traditions, from Taoism and Aboriginal art to shamanic journeying and sitting with the Basarwa in the Kalahari Desert, is rich. And nature herself has been my most important teacher. As a consequence, I find myself returning to the imagery and knowledge held in the web of indigenous traditions from around the world. These traditions honor and celebrate the *whole* interconnected web of life—human, plant, animal, and mineral. Separating the good of the individual from the good of the whole—including the planet itself—is not an option in their way of seeing the world. In these traditions, rich with symbol, ritual, and ceremony, there exist many valuable images pointing toward a true and wholistic way of understanding our place in the larger order of things. One image in particular has served as a steady anchor for much of my adult life, the Native American experience of Seven Directions.

In all honesty, I don't remember when I first encountered this way of understanding the world. It seems as though it has always been with me, nested somewhere deep inside as a kind of "moral compass," a way of understanding the ancient and timeless laws that govern life on planet Earth. Over the years it has served as a steady guide for how I live, make choices, and contribute. When it came to writing this book, there was no other way I could see of describing the path we all need to walk. Therefore, I have selected this way of understanding as a guiding roadmap, offering readers a potential gateway into a worldview leading us back to rather than away from one another. Leading back to connection with the earth and ultimately back to the deepest essence of ourselves. Having chosen this way of viewing the world, I want to be really clear that this book is a distillation of my own study, personal experience, and ongoing interpretation of these ideas. I am not speaking on behalf of any tradition or cultural legacy. Many wise and articulate individuals from a wide range of traditions have deep wisdom to share. If you find yourself drawn to this way of understanding the world, I encourage you to explore further. I have included some starting points of reference in the Appendix.

As a roadmap for your journey into a world of intercon-nectedness, the image of Seven Directions offers landmarks and clues guiding you in the general direction of this inten-tion. Although these landmarks are helpful, they are only landmarks. All the color, vibrancy, momentary beauty, and unexpected detours come about only on the journey itself. Therefore, think of this book as "directional versus prescrip-tive," pointing toward an experience with a few key starting ideas. This is done for one simple reason: The answers to all your questions live inside you. They cannot be given to you by someone else—no matter how often people try to do this for us or we try to find the wisdom we are seeking "out there."

Leadership Flow is a path to be walked—and with deliberate pausing, wondering, experimenting and walking on again.

Guide for Living

Laid out in three parts, the book begins with *Part One: Stepping Stones*, which describes Leadership Flow as a path accessible to all, bringing calm and mutual respect to a world sorely in need of both. Each of us has the capacity to experience Leadership Flow, yet this can take some doing for us modern humans, born and bred into a culture pulling us out of touch with ourselves, each other, and the wider world at every turn. Part One concludes with an explanation of each of the Seven Directions as both metaphor and, for many cultures, as key components of a distinct worldview.

Part Two: Upright and Rooted, and *Part Three: Dancing with the Winds of Change* form the heart of the book. Each chapter focuses on one of the Seven Directions. The structure for these seven chapters is identical: three key concepts captured in a single word with illustrative stories and italicized subthemes; an Explore, Engage, Experiment activity to help ground and practice each key concept; and a closing reflection called Getting Traction. To help you stay oriented and to remind you of the interconnection between these seven domains of awareness, the following image will be used throughout these chapters. Whenever you are exploring one specific direction it will be highlighted.

Part Four: Rebuilding Community concludes with a reminder that, although the deep, ongoing work of leadership is personal and close in, we are constantly being supported and enlivened by the wider whole. As our elders remind us, we are each here for a reason, and we are all needed.

Collective Intelligence

Designed as a trusted resource and guide, this book gives you tools for accessing wholeness and creating more health, sanity, and well-being in you, your family, your community, and your work life. Living in sync with the larger order of things, unseen resources and new possibilities become visible, and new habits replace old. Using the ideas and practices offered throughout these pages, you will be amazed at the ways your leadership shifts and changes. As close friend and colleague Marian Goodman, who works with community leaders, CEOs, and teams around the world, describes, "There is a kind of magic and collective intelligence accessible when all of these skills come together. Everyone feels it, and it is an experience so completely natural and yet so completely different than the more traditional ways of working." If this kind of magic is of interest, open up this little book and see what wisdom it has to share.

PART ONE:

Stepping Stones

Chapter 1:

Leadership Flow

○∞∞∞∞∞∞∞∞∞∞∞∞∞∞∞∞∞∞∞∞∞∞∞∞∞○

"The things that make you strange are the things that make you powerful."
—BEN PLATT, TONY AWARD WINNER, DEAR EVAN HANSEN

*B*ud French[1] is a local farmer who lives in the next town over and delivers hay for our horses. Every three or four months his truck arrives, and we talk about all manner of things, from the spring maple syrup run to local events and national issues. Effortlessly flipping fifty-pound bales of hay into the back of my shed, Bud is the kind of person who inspires me to take myself less seriously, stay in shape, and give thanks for the blessings of this deliberately chosen rural lifestyle. I've come to rely on his advice, not just on caring for and feeding our horses but also on a variety of other questions like who to hire to renovate a falling-down garage or where to find a home for a stray cat. When Bud drives away, I've almost always learned something new, have a smile on my face, and know for certain in good times or bad he is someone I would immediately turn to in search of creative solutions.

I'm not alone. It turns out Bud's the go-to guy for lots of people. He's not my boss, and he's not the mayor of his small town, but when we need someone we trust, he's the one we call. Whether in his role as local fire chief or stopping to help a stranger in need, Bud instinctively walks the path of *Leadership Flow*.

> *Leadership Flow is a way of life that builds wisdom, character, and assurance from the inside out—and from the outside in.*

Bud has realized a potential I believe is within us all. His work with the land and animals constantly enhances the health and well-being of his surrounding community. Never in a rush, he stays solidly in the moment, taking time to listen and connect. And he has no choice but to move with the ebb and flow of the natural world around him. His way of living and leading is one innately known by those who live close to the land, but often forgotten by leaders in our modern culture. There is much to learn about life and leadership from people like Bud, as well-known author Louis L'Amour describes in *The Lonesome Gods*: "Our world is one where the impossible occurs every day, and what we often call supernatural is simply the misunderstood . . . the poor peasant, the hunter, or the fisherman may have knowledge that scholars are struggling to find."[2]

Be Yourself

Bud doesn't wake up in the morning thinking about how he might inspire others; he thinks about the work he wants to do on his farm. He makes plans for his day and adjusts them given changes in the weather or a request to bring one of his farm critters to visit cancer patients at the local hospital. Farming and horses are his callings, whether that means bringing back to life fields that have long stopped producing or training up a new Morgan to escort a local bride and groom to their wedding. It's not that his life is easy, but because his passion, skills, and work are aligned with his calling, excellence in his job, continued self-education, and peace of mind come naturally. His deep authenticity inspires immediate trust and confidence.

Work that resonates with our skills and aptitudes is key to the path of Leadership Flow. As children, we expressed our aptitudes without even thinking about it. Some of us had our noses buried in books; others happily took apart mechanical objects. My sister—now a doctor—constantly wore a nurse's hat and blue cape a la Florence Nightingale. I was the wild child, running around outside in the woods most of the time. Our bodies recognize the activities at which we will excel—those that light us up and allow our inherent leadership skills to emerge. The end product is confidence, born from mastering exactly the things we love to do.

Does this mean we'll never be challenged? Absolutely not. But the challenges faced as we hone our talents differ from other challenges in a significant way. Mainly, we don't dread them. We're drawn to them. They give us a chance to test our strengths and keep improving, to learn new skills, and to make significant contributions to our organizations and communities. Such challenges feel very different from those we face when our work is out of sync with our innate strengths. Work mismatched to our nature or born out of others' expectations can feel like a giant boulder we must push up a steep hill. Tension will build when this is the case, eventually leading to restlessness, anxiety, and depression.

As Emerson reminds us, "To be yourself in a world constantly trying to make you be something else is the greatest accomplishment." Staying true to yourself and steering a course where your unique talents are offered on behalf of the whole is a life-long journey and yet one we all must take seriously.

Leadership Is a Team Sport

Leadership Flow isn't only about us individually; it's also about us collectively. As in the natural world, where healthy ecosystems have a broad range of species doing their exact and specific jobs to create long-term sustainability, we inhabit an interconnected web of humanity relying on everyone's contribution, skills, and expertise. Even for seemingly simple tasks like selecting what mix of hay to feed my horses each year, Bud and I work as a team. He shares his knowledge of the quality of each season's different cuts of hay and how they might affect the animals, and I bring my deep understanding and observation of my horses' unique needs. Together, we keep them healthy and thriving.

Knowing it takes a broad range of skills and aptitudes to get any kind of work done effectively, we can think in terms of healthy ecosystems when it comes to creating organizations where people can grow and flourish. Doing this well, however, often requires profound shifts in the normal ways of understanding leadership. Right up to his heart attack at age thirty-six, David Marsing was working full throttle to pull a microchip fabrication plant out of crisis. Buying into the mind-set that Intel's employees are homogeneous cogs in the insatiable machine, he demanded superhuman contributions from both himself and his teams. The heart attack was David's wake-up call. His brush with death radically changed his perspective—and increased Intel's profits. After much soul-searching, he realized the people he worked with were all forced to "live a kind of lie, caught between who they were and who they had to be . . . and it was destroying their lives." When the call came to be the plant manager of a soon-to-be constructed Fab 11 factory, David accepted the challenge but with a totally new sense of purpose: to design a team operating system based on diversity of expertise, where the key metric for success was the health and well-being of all employees. One of his key observations was, the more disparate the experiences and skills of team members, the more adaptable and dynamic the organization. However, this is not the goal of most companies. They want homogeneity, 150 trumpets playing in unison. But homogeneous teams have blind spots; they move like a herd and often in the wrong direction. What's needed instead is complexity, the team as a jazz ensemble able to both harmonize and improvise.[3]

David not only maximized profits for Intel, he created an environment of healthy, motivated employees who were allowed to be themselves, get behind the larger corporate vision, and have room to create. Before he could accomplish these results, however, David had to make deep and long-lasting shifts in his own habits, mindsets, and ways of living. After his heart attack, David spent several months in recovery. During this period, his cardiologist asked him what kind of work he was doing. After hearing about the nature of the job, the doctor asked, "Did you ever consider a different career?" David said yes, he had thought about being a forest ranger or a university science librarian. His doctor then suggested he become a librarian! During the next year David searched for and eventually found himself a spiritual teacher. Focused on developing a deep practice of meditation, this time helped reframe his approach to his life and specifically his work. Assuming he might take up a less stressful occupation, he explored seriously the idea of a long-term retreat and period of study. His teacher, a Tibetan scholar and meditation master, planted a different seed. Reminding him of the

Tibetan meditation vows he had taken to help other people first, his teacher suggested he ponder how the new factory manager's job could enable David to help relieve the suffering of thousands of people and their families as well as help them see their true potential. Doing the math—five thousand employees, their families, and the larger community—David calculated the number of people directly impacted by this factory would be about twenty thousand. Reframing the opportunity in this way, he decided to return to Intel. Back he went, bringing his inherent talents for navigating the fast-paced nature of this business environment: a physicist trained to measure, observe, and create feedback systems which solve problems, an insatiable desire to question assumptions, and deep confidence dealing with the unexpected and apparently intractable. And he now had his meditation practice firmly in place, allowing him to remain calm and centered in the midst of this intensity.

Traversing new and unchartered territory inside himself was the first step in his journey toward skillfully creating a healthy and sustainable environment for others. This is true for each one of us and is why the path of Leadership Flow begins with self. With one critical caveat, however: It is a "self" squarely situated as a part of a wise and intelligent whole:

> *If you are alive, you are connected to everything else that is alive . . . This is the taproot that underlies all sustainable endeavors—we are all connected . . . If you truly know this, you can never feel lonely.*
> —BOB RANDALL, YANKUNYTJATJARA ABORIGINAL ELDER[4]

Experiencing yourself as a part of an integrated whole is the taproot out of which mastering the challenges and dilemmas of the human experience becomes possible. Without this taproot, the journey of self-discovery becomes partial at best.

Self-Mastery as a Taproot to the Whole

Leadership Flow is rooted in self-mastery, and self-mastery can be learned. Embracing your natural skills and instincts immediately connects you to the deeper universal intelligence coursing through your very bones. With this as a starting point, the task becomes learning how to "course correct" when emotions, egos, or wishes cloud your judgment. Trusting fully in the stable, solid place within anchoring you to the universe, the very things you need to learn will come right to your doorstep. *You don't need to go searching, you simply need to accept the daily and momentary challenges as intelligent and personally selected opportunities for growth and skill building.* In this sense, the urge to leap over the immediate circumstance in favor of something you imagine is better, more important, more significance, or simply more fun has to be tempered. There will inevitably be things needing to change, shift, and adapt. The issues are often about when, where, why, and how you discern the right and accurate path of action. The primary task at hand is how you handle each moment as it lands in your life.

Leadership Flow emerges through the awareness that the most fundamental point of leverage—the solution to most dilemmas—is inside ourselves, not in others. When we make a shift in what we're contributing to any situation, everything around us begins to pivot.

This is easier said than done. Acting authentically daily takes courage, optimism, and a willingness to embrace our shortcomings as well as our assets. We don't learn to listen to our bodies and the world around us for directional clues overnight, and it takes plenty of practice to bravely stop and wait for a cue before acting or responding. The good news is we don't have to reinvent this wheel. The tools for self-mastery were discovered long ago and can be used again and again to move forward with authenticity and confidence. In fact, they are always with us, but we have forgotten how to use them. To remember, we turn to our ancestors for guidance.

Seven Directions of Self-Mastery

Most indigenous cultures—both those that are extant and those that are, sadly, extinct—incorporate the worldview that wisdom and guidance for how to be in the world comes to us through each of either four or seven directions. The directions are both real—North, South, East, West, and sometimes Above, Below, and Within—and metaphorical. Leadership Flow is the *momentary and dynamic engagement with these seven directions.* An unconventional way of understanding the world where possibilities not currently in view reside and can be accessed.

Leadership Flow requires us to see and experience ourselves, other people, and the world itself with fresh eyes. Like Bud and David, we must learn to find new and creative options to the challenges that arise daily. Bud must listen, honor, and work with the cycles and seasons of weather to bring in his annual hay harvest. David had to listen to, honor, and work with a diverse and nuanced range of human capacities to build a healthy and sustainable workplace. Listening, responding, and adapting continually to the ever-shifting conditions of the world connects the power and wisdom of our gifts to the long-term sustainability of the whole. Operating from this place, we can find solutions to the myriad serious and daunting leadership issues we face.

Instead of trying to control or fix yourself or the world, use the Seven Directions as a way to shift your perspective and find your place in the larger whole. Become aware of the dynamic balance between inner stillness and outer effectiveness, where *self, the moment, and the universe work together.*

As a way of illustrating these ideas in action, let me share a story about retrieving twenty bright blue, fifty-pound duffle bags that had gotten stuck in a storage shed in Helsinki, Finland. I'll tell you about this experience, and about each of the Seven Directions, in the next chapter.

Chapter 2:

Seven Directions of Self-Mastery

O⋙⋙⋙⋙⋙⋙⋙⋙⋙⋙⋙⋙⋙⋙⋙⋙O

"To go north, you must go south. To reach the west, you must go east. To go forward, you must go back. To touch the light, you must pass beneath the shadow."
—GEORGE R.R. MARTIN, *A DANCE WITH DRAGONS*

*O*n my first trip to the Soviet Union, in 1986, I was leading a group of young Americans to join their Russian peers for a month-long mountaineering adventure in one of the first US–USSR youth exchanges. The cold war was just beginning its thaw. No direct flights existed between the United States and the Soviet Union (USSR), so our group had a full-day layover in Helsinki. Exhausted and ready for much-needed sleep, we arrived at ten pm at Sheremetyevo airport outside Moscow. Booked on an eight o'clock flight the next morning to the Caucasus Mountains, we knew a small amount of sleep would be better than none at all.

As luggage began dropping onto the carousel, not one of our twenty-two bright blue duffel bags filled with climbing gear was showing up. A wave of nausea rolled through the pit of my stomach. Somehow the bags had gotten stuck in

Helsinki. As I connected eye-to-eye with Becky, my colleague and co-leader, the worry and concern in her stare spoke volumes. Having traveled to the USSR the previous year, her horror stories were endless about the difficulties of accomplishing even the most basic of activities, let alone figuring out to how to retrieve luggage misplaced in another country.

The very real possibility we might be stuck in Moscow for a number of days began to crystalize in my awareness, and I could see Becky resigning herself to this fate. Instead of joining her story and going down into that rabbit hole, I took the only action I could see at the moment. Shuffling everyone out of the terminal, I put them on our prearranged bus and sent them off to the hotel.

Back inside the terminal, I wandered around for a moment and found a place to sit down. In a space absent of all amenities except restrooms, the single plastic chair was a welcome sight. By now it was close to midnight, and the place was virtually empty. Settling into the quiet, I took some slow, deep breaths and my whole body began to relax. For some reason, I was still holding the Lufthansa envelope with all the bag tags in it. As my mind went still, I found myself slowly slapping the palm of my hand with that envelope. Dropping my gaze to the bright yellow envelope, I noticed a list of phone numbers on the back. My eyes raced down the list and spotted a number in Helsinki. "Bingo!"

Jumping out of the chair, I scanned the airport for another human being, anyone who could help me. A security guard caught the corner of my eye. Scurrying up to him, I began tapping my finger on the Helsinki phone number and in broken Russian trying to communicate I needed a phone. Unable to shake me, the guard gave up and led me through a series of hallways to a tiny back office. I handed him the envelope, and he dialed the number. After what seemed an eternity of ringing, a voice finally came on the line. Not only was it a real person, she spoke English! Assuring me she'd look into it and get back to me, she began to say good-bye. "Don't hang up!" I said emphatically, "It is impossible for you to get back to me. I'll stay on the line for as long as it takes to find those bags and be sure they get loaded on the next flight to Moscow."

Tipping his head toward the door, the guard signaled he was leaving to return to his other duties—whatever these were in the middle of the night in an empty airport. I rested my elbows on the desk, cradled my head in one hand and the phone in the other, and listened to the quiet line. Thirty minutes later, the airline representative returned to the phone. The bags had been located in a storage shed, used for long layovers. Now loaded on the first morning flight, they would be headed to Moscow shortly. This flight would arrive with just enough time to make our connection to the Caucasus Mountains. After thanking her profusely, I hung up the phone.

With three hours to spare, I caught a quick snooze on the linoleum floor not far from baggage claim. Early the next morning, the students arrived in time to help me pull the bags off the luggage carousel and race them over to our departing flight. With the bags safely loaded, I turned my attention to the real task at hand, finding a strong cup of tea and breathing a sigh of relief.

Ancient Wisdom

As the first of a long and continuous series of moments where challenges arose with seeming impossible odds of resolution, the summer of 1986 in the USSR taught me to let go and trust the ancient wisdom embedded in the Seven Directions. Dynamic and interactive, the Seven Directions are most easily illustrated with a concrete story highlighting the practical and grounded nature of this kind of leadership. Retrieving the duffel bags will serve as this illustrative example, and will be used to "unpack" each direction one at a time.

Before diving into individual directions, a word on how the directions are "clustered together" is of value. There are two axes: the vertical axis of Being and the horizontal axis of Doing. Three directions reside in the vertical axis of being and the other four reside in the horizontal axis of doing. Imagine these two axes as distinct yet always in a dynamic interaction with each other, *oscillating between how you BE and what you DO*. Hence the term Leadership Flow. With leadership most often equated with taking outer action, the axis of Being may feel less familiar than the axis of Doing. See for yourself which directions feel most accessible and which feel truly foreign. There are no right answers, only starting places for your own exploration and discovery. Linking the directions directly back to the story of the duffel bags, let's see what they look like when put into practice. As I mentioned in the prologue, from here on the following image will help you stay oriented to the seven directions and will show which direction is being discussed by highlighting this part of the image.

The Vertical Axis of Being

Embracing and embodying the Axis of Being brings the focus of attention squarely into the *now*—the moment where everything unfolds. Reviewing the past or worrying about the future are the two primary ways we take our attention away from whatever is happening *right now*. Contrary to some ideas of Being as a place of serenity, tranquility, and the absence of chaos, every moment is filled with virtually infinite possibility, potential, and creativity. Without this axis, we often live in a state of being overwhelmed, never knowing what choice to make when, often feeling any action taken doesn't seem to have lasting impact. Living with a conscious attention to the Axis of Being, our experience of time shifts. Perception sharpens, and choices become more obvious. Anchoring our lives to the now gives access to an intelligence deeper and wiser than our own singular experience. Harnessing this energy and using it with precision becomes the practice. Above, Below, and Within are the three directions that make up this axis.

Above: Trust Life

Above is the direction of honoring, surrendering to, and embracing the vast matrix of creative intelligence holding all of creation. In the travel story, this direction is illustrated by my immediate surrender to the reality of the situation and the clear perception those bags had been stored somewhere out of sight. No judging it as right or wrong, good or bad. This awareness did not make me panic; it made me curious. *I wonder what life has in mind now? Where's the thread of connection to this larger intelligence that might assist?*

At no moment did I feel alone. There was a sense of assurance somehow this would all work out—the universe had my back and was there supporting me. My job was to let go and listen for the one next step—one thing connecting me to something or someone beyond this airport. And in the 1980s in the USSR, there were no cell phones, no English signs, no customer service representatives. Signing onto to Wi-Fi for answers was not an option. I had to connect with my own internal broadband. In some respects, this kind of intelligence was easier to hear back then because no intervening technology could be used as a substitute. Clear insight was received directly.

Accessing this deep intelligence requires acknowledging in a very core way *we are not in control* of unfolding events. We are not God. Trying to play God will get us in trouble every time. What we can control is the way we interact with the events as they unfold. Paradoxically, deliberate and disciplined engagement with the moments coming our way impacts the quality of the moments coming. Further exploration of this paradox, along with a deeper dive into each direction follows immediately from this brief summary of the directions. On to the direction of Within.

Within: Anchor to the Present

Living in the now and handling each situation with integrity and precision is the practice of Within. Creating an internal experience of quiet readiness, a relaxed alertness, is key. Out of this place of readiness, it is possible to discern the first step of action. Prior to the first step, however, there is always a pause, whether milliseconds or minutes. In my story, this direction is illustrated when I find the chair, sit down, and relax with a quiet curiosity and openness to discover what would come next. In this situation, my mind was completely empty. I was waiting. I was listening for some spark of awareness to come. *What is mine to do here? What is someone else's part? What is my first step?*

Once I'd found a quiet place, the Helsinki phone number jumped off the ticket envelope. Voila! First step revealed. In 2021 where cell phones allow you to call anytime from anywhere, the game-shifting experience of noticing a phone number may seem like a real stretch of imagination. The point is remembering all those moments in your own life where *clear, unfiltered insight dropped into a quiet, empty space inside you!* Will 99 percent of the people around you have any idea of the game-changing insight you just received? Most likely not. You do, however, and that's what matters. You know it, and you know you need to act on it. Go empty, pause, and wait for insight. This is the direction of Within. And it dances deeply with the next direction, Below.

Below: Respect Creation

Below is the direction of deep respect for life. The well-known verse, "Whatever you do to the least of my brothers, so do you do unto me," (Matthew 25:31–46) speaks to this direction as long as you expand the definition of "least" to include all forms of life—plants, animals, rivers, mountains, oceans, deserts—*all of creation.* Including all of creation, not just people, distinguishes this direction and signals a truly different path of leadership. Definitions of success and effectiveness expand to include all aspects of your living. What you do at home matters as much as what you do at work. It is all one, an integrated whole. As a friend once suggested, "Before you decide about a life partner, see how they treat their pets."

In my story, the clearest example of Below was the interaction with the security guard. Bureaucracy was huge and multilayered during the mid-eighties in the Soviet Union. Nothing moved quickly through official channels, and the most common response to a question about getting something done was, "It's impossible." The only person I saw at the airport that evening was the security guard. Approaching him as a fellow human being who might be able to help me with a tricky situation rather than as a security guard with no power or influence made an instant impression. Quickly, his hesitation and resistance to help dissolved. Not only did he figure out how to place the call, he was there the next morning to see the bags arrive. As I caught his eye when we began wheeling the bags away, he actually smiled—a true rarity in the context of the Cold War and the deep wariness toward all things American.

Reaching across the barriers of culture, history, and tradition with the people we meet is a doorway into the direction of Below. Expanding the doorway to include every living form on the planet takes a lifetime. Holding the idea that there might be value in cracking the doorway slightly wider than before is what matters. Imagine the creative possibilities of this vastly wider network when it comes to acting in the world, which is the horizontal axis we will now explore.

The Horizontal Axis of Doing

Anchored to the Axis of Being, the horizontal Axis of Doing includes both action and non-action—the awareness of when it's time to do something overtly and when it's time to wait and be still. Made up of the four directions—East, South, West, and North—the outcomes are flexibility, resilience, clarity, and impact. Whereas the axis of Being may seem somewhat invisible or intangible, these directions are much more familiar and recognizable. Relating directly to the key capacities of human experience—heart, body, mind and spirit—we will explore these four directions in this order.

East: Heart: Emotional Agility

The heart is our physical connection to the subconscious "sea" of humanity. As such, it functions much like the ocean—sometimes calm, often stormy, moving with the slightest hint of wind (thoughts stir up the heart). *Riding*

the waves of deep emotion without becoming completely disoriented is the practice of Heart. In our story example, the biggest challenge to my heart was the anxiety and fear that I sensed in the other leader, Becky. Picking up on others' feelings is a useful skill in terms of empathy and awareness. Problems arise when we take on their feelings and act as if they are ours. Asking Becky to go with the group rather than remain with me allowed me to care for both her needs and those of the group. It also gave me the chance to be quiet and relax.

Befriending our emotional intelligence and integrating this intelligence into the choices we make is the gift and challenge of the direction of Heart. And our hearts speak most clearly when our bodies are healthy, strong and well rested.

South: Body: Physical Resiliency

Assuming all things are linked, our physical bodies are directly connected to and in constant communication with the universe itself. Tending and caring for our bodies is one concrete and specific way of tending and caring for the whole. They are one piece of the cosmos for which we are individually responsible. Remembering this and fully inhabiting our bodies allows us to receive the wisdom and intelligence being sent our way. The wave of nausea and sinking feeling in the pit of my stomach was this direction getting my attention. Noticing the sensation in my gut, I acknowledged to the wider universe I had received the message. On the wings of this acknowledgement came the clear perception that the bags had been forgotten and were out of sight.

More often than not, we drag our bodies around without much thought or attention. They plod silently along like a child who has given up trying to communicate her needs, until she decides she's had enough, and then she'll rebel. Rebellion often shows up as physical illness or disease. *Turning toward our bodies' signals, sensations, and information well before full-on rebellion kicks in is the practice of this direction.* And many of the early signals will be about keeping our fuel tanks full, so we have the energy and resiliency needed to form accurate perceptions. These perceptions come most clearly through a mind that knows how to go quiet and receptive.

West: Mind: Mental Fluidity

Relaxation comes to the mind when its stories and machinations are held in a field larger than the mind itself. Like the heart and the body, our thoughts are a piece—a very tiny piece—of the intelligence of the whole. Assuming the stories we tell are the truth with a capital "T," we quickly create a prison of our own making. When the bags didn't appear, everyone began telling stories, assuming we'd be in Moscow for at least several days and worrying about our Russian counterparts already waiting for us in the Caucasus Mountains. The last thing I needed was to hear twenty-one versions of what might happen next. I needed to keep my attention on the present situation without letting my mind wander off toward outcomes I didn't want. Sending everyone off to the hotel meant their stories went with them, freeing me up to *let my mind go empty and be available for insight and possible direction.* This is the practice in the direction of the West.

Letting the stories go and engaging directly with what is happening *now,* the mind finds a place of quiet—just as a lake becomes tranquil when the wind dies down. Into these calm waters, new insight drops like a stone and its message is heard loud and clear. Insights of this kind are characterized by very simple language. In the duffel bag story, "Call the Helsinki Airport" was the phrase that set in motion all the actions needed to recover the bags and bring my group safely to the Caucasus. Arriving at our base camp in a high mountain valley, we met our Russian counterparts at dinner as planned. This is Leadership Flow in action, working day and night to ensure we stay in sync with our spiritual destiny and calling.

North: Spirit: Spiritual Destiny

Knowing our lives have purpose and meaning simply because we were born is the work of spiritual destiny. Imagine a kind of invisible DNA that causes our cells to vibrate with enthusiasm when our choices line up with our natural talents. Steady signals coming from our bodies, minds, and hearts gently guide us toward and away from certain paths and possibilities. One step at a time, listening, experiencing, and making subtle adjustments. Destiny, as I am describing, is not so much a predetermined fate as it is a *dance with the universe to live your highest potential*. The predetermined part is the fact that you are born with certain innate skills and attributes. The dance is how you continually choose to bring these to life. Sometimes these choices seem totally random until the day arrives where the very skills we gathered become critical for our success. Such was the case for me as a teenager when I was drawn to study Russian.

In my small, rural high school in central Vermont, the French teacher was Russian by birth. On a bit of a spontaneous whim, she got permission teach Russian, a true anomaly in the 1970s. With an innate love of foreign languages, I was one of the first to sign up for the class. Who would have imagined a decade later these three years of basic Russian would be key is letting me follow my unfolding destiny? Although my mountaineering expertise was what qualified me to lead this multicultural youth exchange program for Outward Bound, my Russian allowed me to navigate the USSR at a time in history when there was no English spoken or written anywhere.

Taking Russian classes in my youth was an unknown piece of preparation for a future direction. Following threads of genuine interest, regardless of whether they make immediate sense, is how you stay connected to your destiny. *Trusting the momentary choices and not passing judgment when the path seems murky or unclear is the practice.* Anchoring your daily activities to all Seven Directions puts you squarely in the midst of Leadership Flow.

In Practice

One of the ironies of being in Leadership Flow is when events unfold, it often seems as though nothing particularly unusual has occurred. Although the group was expressing concerns about the lost baggage when they left the airport, when they returned the next morning, they weren't surprised to see their bags. Only Becky, who had previous experience of the supreme challenges involved in working in the USSR at that time in history, was genuinely surprised. At the sight of the twenty-two duffel bags stacked on carts ready for our connecting flight, she heaved a sigh of relief. Raising her eyebrows, she looked my direction. I smiled and heaved a sigh of relief too.

On the plane flying south, the significance of what had occurred registered in my bones. A deeper sense of trust and an extraordinary experience of gratitude arose. As life would have it, the duffels were the first test of many. Perpetual challenges, often appearing insurmountable, were part of almost every day for the next three months. I was tested over and over again. The bigger the test, the more anchored I became to the *now*, listening for only the *one next step* to take. Stopping, breathing, I learned there was such a thing as Leadership Flow. The more I practiced, the more aware I became of what I was doing and what I was not doing: rushing to action, worrying about what was next, blaming or criticizing those around me. The summer of 1986 started a lifelong inquiry into what it takes to sync up with the larger order of the universe—to be *connected*. An inquiry anchoring me ever more firmly to the wisdom and beauty of the Seven Directions. With this chapter as an overview, let's dive into each one in depth beginning with the Axis of Being and the three directions that compose it.

PART TWO:

Upright and Rooted

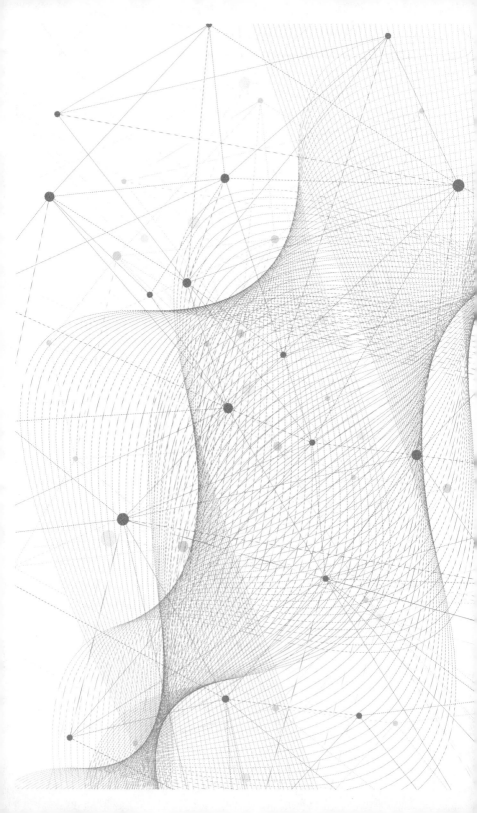

Chapter 3:

How You *Be* Versus
What You *Do*

*"Non-action is unceasing activity. The sage is charac-
terized by a stillness akin to the apparent stillness of a
fast, rotating gyroscope."*

—RAMANA MAHARSHI

Good music is defined by the space between the notes—the
pauses create its depth, power, and impact. Such is the
case with leadership—the practice of non-doing allows action
when it is taken to be powerful and purposeful. A beautiful
example of this kind of power and stabilizing influence was

recently highlighted in a TV series entitled *The Crown*, a docudrama about the life of Queen Elizabeth II. One episode depicts the Great Smog of 1952, in which a cloud of pollutants enveloped London for five days and caused thousands of deaths. Once it lifts, Elizabeth is seen talking with her grandmother, Queen Mary of Teck:

> **Elizabeth:** *What if the fog hadn't lifted? And the government had continued to flounder? And people had continued to die? And Churchill had continued to cling to power? And the country had continued to suffer? It doesn't feel right, as head of state, to do nothing.*
> **Mary:** *It is exactly right.*
> **Elizabeth:** *Is it? But surely doing nothing is no job at all.*
> **Mary:** *To do nothing is the hardest job of all, and it will take every ounce of energy that you have.*

Doing nothing *is* "the hardest job of all." It goes against the grain. We are much more familiar with phrases like "Don't just stand there, do something!" Mary of Teck is right, it often takes "every ounce of energy you have" to stop and *be*. To stand still for a moment before leaping into action. In the case of Queen Elizabeth, her role requires she "do nothing," deliberately not choosing sides or displaying emotion in any particular direction. Her role is to hold all parts of the issue and be a stabilizing presence for others who are tasked with discerning a path of action. At our core, this is a role we all need to play and with much greater frequency, both when empowering others and empowering ourselves. In the words of Peter Morgan, London-born playwright and screenwriter of *The Crown*, "She doesn't say anything, she doesn't do anything, but they're not in a hurry to upset her. She's a pretty powerful character in her silence."[1]

The queen is not the only one who has power in her silence; we all do. Silence and non-action are where our deepest and most authentic power resides. Power having nothing to do with our outer position or profession. The power of our presence, our Essential Self—the Self who knows how to *be* as well as how to *do*.

The Essential Self

All three directions on the axis of Being deliberately cultivate the Essential Self. Humberto Maturana, a noted Chilean biologist and spiritual teacher, substitutes the word "love" for Essential Self, describing it as the one human emotion consistently generating productive and intelligent actions. Otto Scharmer coined a new word—presencing—to describe a way of leading anchored in our presence and our ability to be open to the latent potential of the moment. Whatever word you choose, *shifting your focus to Being, cultivating an inner place from which Doing springs forth automatically, is the work of this axis.*

Exploring the power of being versus doing as a leadership practice is not a totally new concept. Tamara Woodbury, CEO of the Girl Scouts Cactus Pine Council based in Phoenix, Arizona, is a case in point. Internationally recognized for her work in leadership, she wrote an article entitled "Leadership: What's Love Got to Do with It?" She asserted "many of our leadership practices are motivated by fear . . . Our work cultures and structures are rooted in fear of some imagined consequence." Turing the mirror from "out there" to "in here," she noticed how much of her leadership and decision-making was embedded in fear.

With courage and disciplined reflection, she began shifting her own behavior first. When fear and attachment to her own authority surfaced, she focused on opening her heart and listening more deeply. Shedding her impulse to find quick answers and fix things, she began to invite others to join her in the questions:

○ What if we base our leadership on a deeper self-awareness, one that observes our state of *being* as well as the actions of our doing?
○ What would it look and feel like?
○ What difference could it make?
○ What if we freed our leadership from systems of power and positioning and instead used our leadership to build collaborative systems that unleash potential?

As she describes, "Others quickly joined me in this new approach . . . We stopped looking for problems and short-term solutions. We began to see the success and potential that was previously invisible to us."[2]

Reflecting with me recently on what she believed were the most significant and lasting impact of these new leadership practices, Tamara said, "The biggest and most difficult shift was within our governance model. Moving the board from a banking and growth mindset—the highest number of girls as the key metric of success—to a service metric based on reaching all girls took ten years. Our mission went from 'serving more girls' to 'serving girls more.' Our numbers have grown exponentially in underserved communities with 68 percent of our girls coming from households with annual incomes below the poverty rate." Equity and access were core principals of the Girl Scouts founder, Juliette Low. Cactus Pine figured out how to first shift mindsets and then quantifiably measure success based on these metrics. Tapping into the power and practices of Being held critical keys to their success and effectiveness.

Above, Below, and Within

Many people associate Being with a kind of passivity, a going with the flow, somehow separated from results and impact. Nothing could be further from the truth. The power of this axis is its vertical nature, anchored in the larger order of intelligence and grounded by concrete actions in the physical world. It is the interplay among all three directions that creates the ability to access the larger matrix of possibility. The image or idea of Being, without anchoring to the realities of Above and Below, is akin to setting a small boat adrift upon an immense ocean with no navigational tools. You will become completely unmoored, stuck in a sea of empathetic connection to everyone and everything—literally swimming in a stream of unconscious reactions to incoming stimulation. For those caught in this experience, it becomes a state of self-indulgence and sensory addiction. This is the fundamental problem with most "self-improvement" programs; they are only about the self, not the self in service to the whole. Honoring all three directions is the way out of this unconscious trap back to our true home. As Albert Einstein describes, without the axis of Being we cannot find our true nature:

> *"Becoming human is the act of making room in oneself for the immensities of the universe. Unless we do so we cannot find our true nature. We will wander in pain and loneliness . . . attaching ourselves to one fragment after another, each taking us further from our center."*[3]

Return to Center

In Hopi legend, finding our way back to our center requires trust in the guiding hand of the Creator and release of orientation in the material world. Guidance was ever-present as long as people kept the tops of their heads open and sang praises to the Creator every single day. Keeping the top of your head open is the symbol for receiving wisdom from Above. Singing praises to the Creator is accomplished through practical action done with a spirit of blessing and gratitude Below. The direction of Within is the present moment where the invisible impulses from the universe meet the world of physical, mental, and emotional form.

Beginning with Above, we now take a deeper dive into some key attributes of each direction.

Chapter 4:

Above: Trust Life

○─∞∞∞∞∞∞∞∞∞∞∞∞∞∞∞∞∞∞─○

"Look at the sky. We are not alone. The whole universe is friendly to us and conspires only to give the best to those who dream and work."

—APJ ABDUL KALAM, FORMER PRESIDENT OF INDIA

Two young fish are swimming along one day, and an old fish swims by and asks, "How's the water, boys?" The young fish automatically respond, "Fine." A minute or two later one of them asks the other, "What's water?"

Dialogos, the consulting company for which I worked, hired an outside expert to help us with market positioning. He told us, "It's your choice. You can either be a shark or a guppy out there, and I don't have to tell you which one comes out on top." I listened for a while and then asked, "What about the ocean that holds them both? That's what I'm interested in." As you might imagine, this comment stopped the conversation. Looking at me with a "What planet are you from?" expression, he finally laughed and went back to his analogy. I was totally serious.

What does it mean to become aware of the *water*? Assuming we are all part of an integrated system in which we are all swimming, talking about the *ocean* becomes relevant. Directly experiencing this sea of dynamic potential and letting it assist you in all endeavors, be they personal or professional, is the practice of Above. A starting point for this direction is Trust.

Trust

As the CEO of an international nonprofit, I felt stuck. After launching two new leadership schools in South Africa and Bulgaria and secured funding for our local Colorado school, the organization was on solid ground. I, however, had run out of creative steam. Frustrated and irritable rather than inspired and upbeat, news of a good consultant came my way. In hope of finding my own mojo again, I made a call and got on her calendar.

Lisabeth listened quietly as I talked. Wrapping up my overview, I looked at her expectantly. Without missing a beat, she said "You're the problem. You need to resign." Shock and indignation came first, followed by a mental list of "reasons" she was wrong. Biting my tongue, I took three deep breaths and asked her to continue. Clearly and without fanfare, she shared the perceptions leading to this conclusion. Much to my surprise, the longer she spoke, the more her thinking made sense. Somewhere in my gut, it all rang true. An unexpected door had opened, one I had not even considered. Mulling over the implications, I left with big questions.

As life would have it, three days later I had an astrology reading. Every year for over a decade, these readings have helped incorporate the movements of the stars into the rhythms of my life. Precisely synchronized with the advice of the consultant, my astrologer said it was time to make a major shift, close a chapter of my life, and move on. And to do it in the next two weeks! Two professionals, sharing perceptions from vastly different worldviews, with the exact same message. Turning away and continuing on with "business as usual" would be a clear signal to the universe I was not listening. The message was clear; the biggest concern was financial.

We had just bought a house, and my husband was launching a new business. My salary was the only steady source of income. Although not huge, it was enough to keep the bills paid. With my husband's support and no clue how to cover this financial gap, I took a leap of faith and resigned. Two weeks later my mother called. "A very strange thing just happened. We heard from our stockbroker that a few years ago when we were in Memphis, some stocks got lost from your account. They are sending you a reimbursement check for seven thousand dollars." My jaw dropped in disbelief, and it turned out to be the exact amount of money we needed to cover the bills until I landed my next job. And this "gift" of money was completely out of character from my frugal parents for whom self-reliance was paramount. The entire scenario was atypical and totally magical in that "let go and let God" kind of way.

Taking the Leap

I am not advocating everyone be as radical as I, leaping off cliffs when your life seems bleak and uninspired. What I *am* pointing to is cultivating a deep trust in a larger intelligence informing your life at home and at work. Taking risks, even when the potential rewards are not entirely obvious, is the edge where your individual life intersects with this magic matrix of potential.

As Goethe so eloquently phrased it:

"Until one is committed, there is hesitancy, the chance to draw back—concerning all acts of initiative (and creation), there is one elementary truth the ignorance of which kills countless ideas and splendid plans: The moment one definitely commits oneself, then Providence moves too. All sorts of things occur to help one that would never otherwise have occurred. A whole stream of events issues from the decision, raising in one's favor all manner of unforeseen incidents and meetings and material assistance, which no man could have dreamed would have come his way. Whatever you can do, or dream you can do, begin it. Boldness has genius, power, and magic in it. Begin it now."

Major leaps of faith have been taken by most everyone I know at least once or twice in their lives. Sometimes we are pushed to the edge of a cliff, and there is literally no other choice but to leap. Other times the leap seems random and very risky. Either way, leaping involves being open to new and creative opportunities. Compelled by our inherent desire to learn and grow, we hope the freefall won't be too long and the universe will create a soft landing. Often this is the case, and we heave a sigh of relief everything worked out fine. The greater challenge can be handling the times when landings are not so soft but instead *appear* hard and disruptive. In these moments, keep trusting and don't second-guess yourself. Don't judge. Stay curious. See what wisdom may be working out in the longer term.

Good, Bad, Who Knows?

An old Chinese farmer had a mare that broke through the fence and ran away. When his neighbors learned of it, they came to the farmer and said, "What bad luck this is. You don't have a horse during planting season." The farmer listened and then replied, "Bad luck, good luck. Who knows?"

A few days later, the mare returned with two stallions. When the neighbors learned of it, they visited the farmer. "You are now a rich man. What good fortune this is," they said. The farmer listened and again replied, "Good fortune, bad fortune. Who knows?"

Later that day, the farmer's only son was thrown from one of the stallions and broke his leg. When the neighbors heard about it, they came to the farmer. "It is planting season and now there is no one to help you," they said. "This is truly bad luck." The farmer listened, and once more he said, "Bad luck, good luck. Who knows?"

The very next day, the emperor's army rode into the town and conscripted the eldest son in every family. Only the farmer's son with his broken leg remained behind. Soon the neighbors arrived. Tearfully, they said, "Yours is the only son who was not taken from his family and sent to war. What good fortune this is. . . ."[1]

Good, bad, who knows? Trusting in life requires letting go of judging. Often the very circumstances typically classified as "bad" are the ones cultivating deep wisdom and resilience. The twenty-seven years Nelson Mandela spent in prison are a case in point. In his autobiography, *A Long Road to Freedom,* instead of viewing these years as wasted and unfortunate, he described them as absolutely critical in cultivating the self-discipline, inner strength, and authority necessary for him to lead South Africa out from under the apartheid regime. He maintained he couldn't have left a day earlier and been able to carry out what was required of him going forward.

Releasing the propensity to judge creates *freedom in* each situation rather than seeking *freedom from* a situation. Standing in this place, one knows deep, personal power, power based inside oneself rather than outside. Connecting to this level of strength is what it means to practice the direction of Above. With this connection, no one can take your power away unless you give it to them.

True Seat of Power

Jody is a statewide organizer for a rapidly growing progressive political movement. Although she loves the work, the myriad of organizational issues plaguing this ever-expanding nonprofit can be truly frustrating. In a recent conversation, I casually asked, "How's it going?"

After a long moment of silence, she sighed and said, "Let's put it this way. I had a talk with my boss this morning and if I could have been diminished, I would have been." Put this phrase on a T-shirt! In a nutshell, it captures the essence of true power. If you can be diminished you will be—in any number of contexts and on any given day of your life. There will always be a steady flow of challenges. And they will come from all directions—above, below, and sideways. The question is, who is in the driver's seat when they come? Are you? Or is the person with whom you are interacting? Do you stay connected to your own seat of power, or do you give it over to the surrounding environment? I believe the universe never brings you a situation you cannot handle. You *do* have what it takes to meet the challenges—you only need to trust yourself and lean in rather than run away. *Trusting life boils down to trusting yourself, your presence, and your place in the universe.* You are here for a reason, and often the reason is simply to show up. Show up in each moment to the best of your ability with all the grace, guts, resilience, and poise you can muster. This is what it means to Trust with a capital T.

When your fists start to clench and your breathing goes shallow, when the direction things are heading is not what you envisioned—take these moments to stop, breathe, and get curious as to what else might be at play. What else is going on? Is the universe trying to get my attention? Is there some new or unseen possibility seeking to arrive on my doorstep if I would but open to it? Although the first reaction may be one of fear or apprehension, there can also be whispers of something new, unusual, or fresh. Lean into the newness instead of running away from it. Take one step in the direction of the universe and see what surprises might unfold.

Explore, Engage, Experiment

Think of a time when you took a true leap of faith. It doesn't have to be a giant leap; small leaps are equally valid. Write down your experience using the following questions as starting points:

- *What happened?*
- *Did you land on your feet, or did it totally derail things? Perhaps both?*
- *What is your actual experience of taking leaps of faith?*
- *Is this something you do or find too risky?*
- *How are your leaps of faith connected to your experience of power?*

The more you leap, the deeper you trust. The deeper you trust, the more you let things unfold rather than make things happen.

Let Go

Trying to finish a project with pressing deadlines, I brought my phone and computer to bed. Although I was running a high fever with bed-soaking sweats, it still hadn't dawned on me I had a serious case of the flu. Around eleven o'clock that night, I got up to go to the bathroom. That is all I remember. As I resumed consciousness, I heard my husband calling 911 and found myself on floor next to the toilet. Evidently, I had called out to him as I began passing out. Grabbing me in the nick of time, he caught me as I fell. Ash gray and totally unconscious, I was out cold and flat on the floor. By the time the EMTs arrived, I could open my eyes but that was it.

In my fifty-eight years of living, I had never had the experience of being in my body but unable to move it. It was truly amazing. There was not one ounce of fear—only supreme curiosity and deep love for the EMTs who got me out of the bathroom, into an ambulance, and to the hospital for intravenous rehydration. Ironically or serendipitously, I'd been contemplating the nature of letting go earlier that week.

Although my example may seem extreme, illness is often our teacher in the art of surrendering to life and letting go. Connected to this larger field of intelligence, our bodies know we are making choices out of sync with a deeper flow. Like me, if we don't pay attention to the early signs, the messages get louder until there is no choice *but* to let go. Listening early and heeding the signals allows the body to correct course and heal quickly. The problem in our modern world is wanting this course correction instantly rather than at a pace the body can accommodate. As one physician wrote, "If people would only wait three days before coming to see me, virtually all their symptoms would have gone away on their own." Speeding things up to meet self-imposed images of success and failure, be it pushing our bodies to heal unrealistically fast or pushing a project out the door before it is fully realized, is a basic, almost unconscious drive for control.

The Urge to Control

The need to feel as if we are in control of our lives is very strong. The thinking process goes something like this: *If I could somehow control my life, I could influence what comes into it, letting in the good parts and somehow keeping out the bad ones.* You can control how you react to what life brings; the part you surrender is thinking you can control the specific and concrete elements of each situation as it unfolds. In an odd kind of paradox, you are both in control and not in control simultaneously. And to complicate matters, handling each situation with care and precision, I believe, influences the kinds of situations coming your way. Assuming we impact the field of creative intelligence with every personal action, the quality of the action is also registering in the larger field. To illustrate, think of a simple interaction with your child or spouse. One of you starts a conversation. The other reacts . . . and then there is a moment of clear choice. What do *you* do next? Do you escalate and amplify the reaction? Do you disengage? What do you do? That is the only and perpetual question to ask. What do *I* do right now? The idea is simple: stay in the moment and engage consciously. Stop yourself from grabbing ahold of old stories and habits, and interrupt what may have become a regular pattern of action/reaction. These are the things you can control. This is where all the leverage lies. The problem is we *so want to control the other person* and what they might choose to say or do. This is what we surrender. Our attempts to control others are, in truth, a distraction from taking full responsibility for ourselves. With the exception of young children, who clearly need parents to help with boundaries and choices, giving back responsibility to others for their lives is the action. Surrendering our need to try to fix or control things—be it people or circumstances—opens the space to fully engage with what IS.

Stay with What Is

Engaging with what *is* instead of wishing things were different is the heart of letting: letting go of preconceived ideas of how life should unfold and letting come the exact circumstances an intelligent universe is delivering twenty-four hours a day. For sure there are times in our lives where things are clear, action is obvious, and we glide along without experiencing a lot of challenge or resistance. More often than not, however, there are times in our lives requiring us to live in what might be called "the gray zone" for long periods. By "gray zone" I mean living in the midst of deep uncertainty in situations which would often be seen as scary and uncomfortable: sudden shifts in our health, a downsizing at work, a sick child, or a dying parent. Embracing these uncertainties instead of trying to make them go away as quickly as possible requires mental and emotional work. It means letting go of stories and fears, including:

- ○ The urge to have the future all figured out in order to not feel afraid of what might happen and if you will be able to handle it
- ○ The scenarios in your own mind of what is a good outcome versus a bad outcome

- ○ The desire to be "right" rather than to reach understanding
- ○ The urge to act—almost any action will do—rather than leaving empty space when the path forward is *unclear*

In these situations, feeling helpless is common. Perhaps there is no more intense training ground for building this muscle of letting go and letting come than working with a parent in the process of dying. I had the unbelievable privilege and challenge of being with my parents as my mother passed away. In early June my mother broke her arm. Although it was a serious injury, none of the family thought this accident was life-threatening. As I was visiting my parents on a regular basis, I left for Vermont on what I assumed it would be a two-day visit to check in. As life would have it, I ended up staying for almost two weeks. My mother went from conscious and communicative to unconscious and in her own deep process. At times she was peaceful, at times highly agitated. I needed to be wholly present and aware of any small momentary actions needed. At one point I had decided to go home for a few days. I packed up my small overnight bag and went to say good-bye. I whispered to Mom, "I am going home for a few days, but I'll be back soon."

Her smile disappeared and deep sadness spread across her features. In a quiet voice she said, "Please don't go."

In my sixty-two years on this planet, my mother had never asked me to do anything for her. Stroking her hair, I whispered, "If you want me to stay, I will stay for sure." She nodded a gentle yes. Back upstairs went my bag. Letting go of any time-frames, I was there for the duration, however long it took.

At one point my husband came up to say his good-byes and as he sat quietly, he kept getting a strong image of my crawling into her bed and lying beside her. Before leaving, he quietly mentioned this. At the time I told him that seemed tricky because she would scream out in pain if you even tried to sit on the edge of the bed. However, in the most critical moments of her process, this was indeed the one action that calmed her. And it was what I felt compelled to do in what turned out to be the last minutes of her life. Crawling into her bed, I slipped her fragile hand in mine and began to sing very softly. My father was sleeping in the bed beside us, and my sisters had gone to get something to eat. As I was singing, I experienced a very vivid image from my childhood. I often had bad dreams and would go downstairs, wake her up, and ask if I could crawl into bed with her. As I held this image, an experience of deep peace, safety, and unconditional love filled the space between us. And on this timeless quality of love between mother and daughter, she left her body, her racing heart stilled, and her breathing stopped.

Very soon after she took her last breath, my younger sister came back. She came over and smiled to think how peaceful we both looked before she realized mom had passed on. She called my other sister over from her house, which was right next door, and the three of us sat for a short while together before waking dad to let him know.

The beauty and mystery of the dying process is truly about both letting go and letting come. Letting come—letting come the impulse to lie beside her, an image I would never have thought of myself because of her previous experience of pain. Yet it became the exact thing she needed. And then, simultaneously, letting her go as her heart slowed and her breathing stopped.

I cannot imagine a more beautiful experience, and it was also intense and "not easy" in that deep, life-altering way. Letting is like this often—beautiful, intense, and not easy. There is no better teacher than the dying process to learn about letting. Each process is unique, has its own timeframe, and is a dance with the deep mystery of life itself. If you can stay engaged with each moment, playing your part, whatever this turns out to be, you will develop the muscles of letting.

At its core, letting is all about trusting life and surrendering to the flow. As the practice of letting gets more real, a true and precious gift comes along: a new sense of stability.

Surrender to the Flow

The stability arises because you are no longer trying to do something completely and utterly impossible, to control life. You are surrendering to the "river of life," to an intimate experience of being carried by forces greater and wiser than you alone. Working with those "gray zone" experiences can help build the confidence to move through the fear of pushing off the banks and being swept fully into the current of the river itself. Learning how to transition from trying to remain seated on the banks of the river rather than fully surrendering to the current of life is the practice of letting. The river is strong, and we are not sure where it might take us. Like a leaf being carried downstream, we have no way of knowing where the river is ultimately headed. Trusting there is wisdom in the flow and it always has your best interests at heart helps you overcome any fear and anxiety that may arise.

Over time the experience of stability in the midst of dynamic motion becomes a real, palpable foundation upon which you can rely and relax. And, you can learn to enjoy the ride and learn how to play in the midst of the current, moving with it rather than struggling against it. Start with relatively simple issues as a point of entry. Carrying on the metaphor of the river, begin where the waters are mostly calm, with "flatwater" issues and work your way up to moments of increased turbulence and intensity. As you build skill, you will find the ability to stay engaged and steady in the midst of big and challenging whitewater rapids.

Explore, Engage, Experiment

Notice all the different ways the urge to control arises. Experiment with releasing your grip on a situation and letting go of a fixed position. You may need to first name any emotions surfacing to honor their validity. Once you have done this, ask the emotion to "sit on the side for the moment." See if you can get to a place of relaxation. Try the following:

- *Name the emotion that arises when you restrain yourself from taking over the situation.*
- *Notice what happens throughout your entire body if you are able to let go completely.*
- *If you cannot let go, ask yourself "What is the worst thing that can happen?"*
- *Notice what is happening in the environment based on your ability to let go or not.*

As the muscles of letting go and surrender increase, the habit of pushing and forcing starts to relax. As this happens, questions often arise about the real and imagined ways you think about time.

Time

With Internet, Instagram, and newsfeeds coming at us 24/7, reclaiming your relationship with time takes serious discipline. In this world of nanoseconds, how do you reconnect with the longer, more cyclical nature of time? Contemplating your use of time is arguably the most important leadership question you can ponder.

How are you spending your time?
On what?
Why?
What is your relationship with time?

Take a moment and think about the story you are telling yourself about time. Are you super busy in your current story? If so, take a look at this. Being busy often gets confused with being effective. When I was an associate professor at Regis University, every time someone knocked on my office door, their opening phrase was "I know you are very busy but . . ." (fill in the blank with some request).

Responding with a smile, I would say, "I'm not busy, what do you need?" Dismissing my comment with a laugh, they would apologize again before making their request. They really couldn't believe I was not busy. I wasn't busy. How about you?

A Badge of Honor

Busy has become a badge of honor. What happens if you take off the badge? Assume you have vastly more influence on your time than you ever imagined. What would you do differently? There is no right answer; there are only real questions to ponder. Often busy is a proxy for the anxiety lurking right below the surface when you slow down a bit. What happens when you slow down? For many, up comes fear and stories about being left behind, not being valued, not being a team player. Look around at the stories of highly successful people and, more often than not, they are very precise in how, where, and with whom they choose to use their time. Time, like money, is an investment. Whatever you focus your time on will grow. It is a reinforcing loop. Focus and commitment in one direction grows that part of your life, inherently taking time away from some other aspect. Contrary to the myth that you can do it all, you can't. Every moment is a choice. One door opens wider and another door begins to close slightly. Short-term choices frequently turn into long-term projects. Be mindful of this reality. Most of us totally underestimate the time and commitment needed to take seed ideas into fully mature products.

Choose Wisely

Seeking a better work/life balance, I took a rather drastic step and adopted two horses. A highly accurate impulse, these thousand-pound companions have brought great joy, along with clear boundaries around too much traveling for work. On my first visit to an equine rescue facility, a three-year-old quarter horse named Inga caught my eye and opened the floodgates of my heart. I adopted her that very day. As herd animals, horses need at least one companion, and the second horse we chose was even younger!

With both the horses and me in serious need of some guidance on how to stay safe and communicate with one another, I hired a trainer. The first of several who came and went during year one, each had an underlying need to "break the horse." Speed and "getting them ridable" were the two dominant models of success. "Give me your horses for thirty days and I guarantee you'll be able to ride them" was the mantra. Turning my horses over to someone for several weeks was a nonstarter. Building my own relationship and communication skills was as important as building these capacities in the horses. Having someone else do all the work and then hand them back to me and my husband didn't make sense. I also didn't want to "break the horses." I wanted them whole and thriving. There had to be an option where we were all learning and growing together. His name was Klaus, and he lived in Denmark.

Early on, Klaus emphasized the huge time and commitment involved in learning to work with horses this way. Drawing an analogy of climbing a steep, virtually unscalable mountain with people who could hardly tie their boots, he asked, "Do any of you really want to scale this mountain?" Most of the ten people in the room raised their hand, including me. Looking around the room his eyes landed on me. Sighing, he said, "Even you, Peri, have no idea what this takes!" He was right. Still blissfully naive, I had no idea of the time and commitment involved. Daily feeding and hauling horse manure is the easy, quick part. What takes time is building a real, trusting relationship. If more than a few days go by and I have not been out with my horses, the relationship dims slightly. And I have only two! Take this to scale in some of your organizations, and the task of building good, solid, strong relationships with a group or team of people is serious, long-term work.

Time and commitment. Today. Tomorrow. The next day. Wise words for virtually any serious endeavor we undertake. Things take longer and demand more of us than we can imagine. With this as a reality, check to be sure your time and energy is invested wisely. Think about the projects you take on or initiate. Are they truly meaningful? Will they keep your focus and commitment long after the initial excitement of something new wears off? If, after careful review, the answer is "no," contemplate what it might take to pivot toward something else. The philosopher Howard Thurman said, *"Don't ask what the world needs. Ask what makes you come alive and go do it. Because what the world needs is people who have come alive."* Aligning our lives around work and hobbies that light us up not only connects us to the whole; it is what gives us the staying power to hang in there, learn, and grow over time.

Time to Learn

Back to my example with the horses. A second big "reframe" from Klaus was this notion that in "thirty days your horse will be ridable." His timeline for young horses like ours was seven to ten years! Not only did they need to develop physically and emotionally like any being, animal or human, but my husband and I had to learn our way toward being skilled horse people. This was the biggest challenge. Ironically, when I heard this reframe, something deep inside relaxed. Finally, I had a realistic sense of what I had intuited right from the start. It takes time to get good at anything; time, discipline and dedication. Imagining my horses and I could become totally skilled and in sync overnight was simply not true.

And there has been one more priceless lesson about time my horses have taught me. No rushing.

No Rushing

Horses are prey animals. If I come to the horses rushed and unfocused, they instinctively become wary and often walk away! I believe this is intuitively true of people as well, but they have been trained to be polite. Horses haven't. They mirror back your internal state precisely, and if you have a real relationship, they simply wait for you to get it together. As soon as you do, they will often walk over and be immediately ready to engage, inviting you into the moment to listen and learn.

Every session takes however long is needed. Sometimes it's five or ten minutes, sometimes we are together for an hour or more. With genuine connection and clear communication, the horses have all the time they need to learn, offering back their best attempts at whatever the task at hand. Perceiving the subtle cues and asking for only one task at a time requires full presence and never being in a hurry. My horses have literally trained me to "be here now." And this training has carried over directly to my effectiveness as both a coach and a consultant.

A Real Relationship

Often the energy of "rushing" is simply because we are not taking responsibility for our relationship with time. Sadly, the unintended consequences of this ingrained habit will, inevitably, wreak havoc. A kind of unconscious destruction so poignantly captured in this old story from *Zorba the Greek*.

> *"I remember one morning when I discovered a cocoon in the back of a tree just as a butterfly was making a hole in its case and preparing to come out. I waited awhile, but it was too long appearing and I was impatient. I bent over it and breathed on it to warm it. I warmed it as quickly as I could and the miracle began to happen before my eyes, faster than life. The case opened; the butterfly started slowly crawling out, and I shall never forget my horror when I saw how its wings were folded back and crumpled; the wretched butterfly tried with its whole trembling body to unfold them. Bending over it, I tried to help it with my breath, in vain.*
>
> *"It needed to be hatched out patiently and the unfolding of the wings should be a gradual process in the sun. Now it was too late. My breath had forced the butterfly to appear all crumpled, before its time. It struggled desperately and, a few seconds later, died in the palm of my hand.*
>
> *"That little body is, I do believe, the greatest weight I have on my conscience. For I realize today*

that it is a mortal sin to violate the great laws of nature.
We should not hurry, we should not be impatient, but
we should confidently obey the external rhythm."²

Such raw and tender power in this story. Running rough-shod over the deeper and inexorable rhythms of creation, we unintentionally do harm. It is sobering to look at all the times in my life I have "made something happen," only to see the chaos and destruction set in motion by my impatience. The invitation is to look squarely at your own version of this habit and ask these questions. Where are *you* trying to force things to happen? Are the timelines you have created artificially imposed? Where can you open up your perception of a situation and embrace a wholly new and much more accurate timeframe?

Imagine time as the most precious gift you have. How are you using it?

Explore, Engage, Experiment

Bring to mind one or two current dreams or aspirations. They can be personal or professional aspirations. Think specifically about the time frame you have attached to these aspirations. Ask yourself the following questions for each aspiration:

- *What was my original goal?*
- *How close am I to achieving it?*
- *Is the timeframe I have put around it realistic, accurate and useful? If so, great.*
- *If not, what timeframe could I use that would allow me to relax and enjoy this pursuit?*
- *Is it still worth doing? If not, what would it take to let go of this direction and create space for something more creative and inspiring to appear?*

Pursing dreams, aspirations, and activities is how we engage with the realities of life. Every moment seeds are planted. Some we tend deliberately, others not so much. The harvest comes in its own season. Surrendering to the arcs of time—be they short or longer than our lifetime—is how we dance with the intelligence of Above, letting it assist and support our work in the world.

Getting Traction

For each of the seven directions, there are telltale signs of Getting Traction in your journey toward active engagement with these ideas. Two experiences signaling progress in embracing the direction of Above are *gratitude* and *synchronicity*.

Gratitude, spontaneous and genuine, is one of the clearest indicators of welcoming the deeper intelligence of life. Notice all the small moments—like arriving on the doorstep of your home safe and sound from a week of travel or leaning into a challenging situation rather than wishing it would disappear. Appreciating things precisely as they are signals to the larger order of things a readiness to dance with whatever shows up in your life. *There are no small moments or big moments; there are only moments. Choosing your response to each one is an art.* When there is openness and curiosity, life can find you more easily and support your endeavors.

In addition, synchronicities appear with greater frequency. You bump into a long-lost friend in an airport because your plane was delayed and you went to find a place to eat. Serious investors come forward to take your product to its next phase of development at exactly the right moment. As Goethe reminds us, *"Providence moves and all sorts of things occur to help one that would never otherwise have occurred."*

Connecting with Above, you surrender to the deep flow of the river where boldness, power, and magic reside.

The primary metric in embracing Above is increased experiences of gratitude and synchronicity. Start tracking how these two aspects of life are showing up.

O As a daily practice:
Name three things for which you feel genuine gratitude today.

O As a monthly reflection:
Write down an example of synchronicity showing up this month.

Chapter 5:

Within: Anchor to the Present

○⊶⊶⊶⊶⊶⊶⊶⊶⊶⊶⊶⊶⊶⊶⊶⊶⊶○

"Give in neither to the past nor the future. What matters is to be entirely present."
— KARL JASPERS, GERMAN-SWISS PHILOSOPHER,
PSYCHIATRIST

A few years ago, a team from Dialogos was brought in to help the United States Forest Service USFS) change their trajectory of annual fatalities. Despite all efforts and a rigorous, agency-wide focus on safety, the annual death toll of employees who found themselves on the front lines fighting fires and out in the field doing research continued to climb.

Initiating an agency-wide conversation, the team uncovered eight underlying dynamics central to creating unsafe behavior. This analysis resulted in new practices including robust dialogue and collective conversations about both the problem and the solution. For these dialogues to be successful, they had to be "leader led", i.e. led by 1,200 leaders from across the agency. Conducting these conversations required teaching this core group to create space for diverse participation and resist the temptation to offer quick answers and pat solutions. Everyone had to deepen their ability to "stand still and do nothing." This was particularly challenging when the conversations hit places of silence. Yet it was precisely in these moments when the groups could be patient and wait, that new insights arose. Structures were created to capture these insights and share them agency-wide.

A critical outcome of this collective conversation process was a deep shift in mindset. Changing the structure of a program previously managed by a small group of safety officers, all employees were issued a Yellow Card. With this card they could stop any situation immediately if they felt things were not safe. Moving responsibility for the safety and well-being from a few safety officers back to the entire workforce made everyone a part of the solution and a caretaker for the safety of the whole.

It's been well over a decade since these initial engagements began. Shortly after this work began, the numbers began dropping from the historical average of eight or nine fatalities a year. With perseverance and the mantra "even one is too many," zero annual fatalities occurred. Sustaining this result is now the work. Collective conversations are the norm, requiring everyone to continue building their ability to "stand still, be present, and listen."

Pause

Learning how to stand still, to pause, is the central practice of Within. It is the Taoist concept of "not doing." By "not doing," we create space—empty space. Staying with this emptiness until the right, next action is known challenges the fast-paced rhythm of most business environments. Yet often it is the only way to break through tough and intractable challenges.

Challenges, particularly thorny and recurring ones, are a sure sign of old habits needing to change. Shifting habits means noticing what you are doing and trying something new. This is virtually impossible if you are not anchored in the present moment—the nanosecond where reflex begins. A step or two behind—or in front—of the moment and the old habit takes over before you notice. Building your pause muscle interrupts life on autopilot, creating the possibility to engage with the person or situation differently.

Pauses can be super short—literally a second or two—or much longer, like Bill Gates's "solo think weeks." As the boss of Microsoft, twice a year, he would escape for a week to a secluded cabin in a cedar forest. Famously, one of his think weeks in 1995 led to an email sent to all executive staff titled "The Internet Tidal Wave," accurately predicting the future of web surfing. This insight caused Microsoft to develop its own Internet browser and defeat its competitor, Netscape. By interrupting his normal pattern of work, Bill created space—space for fresh insights to land and new habits to be created.[1]

Shifting Gears

Taking weeks or days or mornings can all be invaluable as a means of shifting from autopilot to present moment. Deliberately interrupting routines by going to a "neutral place," be it Starbucks, the local park, or a five-minute break in your office where you shut down distractions and simply breathe are versions of this idea. Retraining your brain and body to unplug from the relentless pace and return to the now is akin to learning how to downshift from overdrive. A few beginning lines of reflection are the following:

What would be your version of "think weeks"
or time to "be"?

What does it take for you to "not do"?

*How do you stop, relax, and become receptive to
the possibilities of the moment?*

Like many of the practices in this book, although they are
simple in concept, they are not easy to execute. For starters,
they can feel intensely uncomfortable at all levels—physically, mentally, and emotionally. Back along the way when
this muscle was less developed in me, I would drop into my
airplane seat after a long day of consulting. Rather than read
or eat or do anything externally, I deliberately turned my
attention inward and focused on slowing down. Closing my
eyes and using my breath, I initially had a mini "detox"
experience: my body was jittery, antsy, and ultra-agitated.
Staying present while these physical symptoms subsided took
patience and practice. At some point, I am not sure exactly
when, perhaps five to seven minutes, I would break through
into a place of total calm, dissipating all the angst and agitation. Gradually I learned to stay increasingly present, and the
build-up of excess energy occurred less frequently. In many
ways we live in a culture addicted to speed so the image of
detoxing is an apt one. Unplugging from this addiction takes
discipline and deliberateness. Why do it? What do you get
for your efforts? Two concrete advantages: less stress and
greater precision.

Becoming Mindful

I am not the only one who has figured out this connection
between speed and stress. The surge in meditation and mindfulness practices across all sectors and industries is a direct
result of this search for strategies to unplug from the fast
pace and destress from feeling overwhelmed. Mainstream

business publications now regularly feature articles on these practices and the impact there are having, for example, the *Wall Street Journal Online* article "Meditation Brings Calm to CEOs."[2] Being the place of calm in the midst of the storm is a leadership function. Calm arises from being present in the now. Meditation and mindfulness are ways of building this place of calm, the muscle of returning to center, a muscle often gone weak from lack of exercise. The more you practice it, the more automatic it becomes. And one of the primary pathways of practice is to focus on your breathing.

Explore, Engage, Experiment

The simplest way of increasing your capacity to be present is to use your breath. Practice taking three breaths—three long, deep, breaths. Pause for a moment in between each breath and notice the gradual relaxation that settles in your body.

- *Whenever you find yourself running out ahead of the present moment, bring yourself back by taking three deep breaths.*
- *Notice what happens inside yourself and in the outer circumstance after you have taken three breaths.*

Using three breaths is a simple and effective method for anchoring yourself in the moment and not rushing to fill the space prematurely. It creates a kind of pregnant pause—a place of readiness that can be held as long as needed until a direction of action becomes clear.

Readiness

A field of readiness is the natural by-product of pausing and focusing wholly in the present. Out of this field of readiness, the impulse to act arises spontaneously and flows directly without thought or hesitation. A colleague of mine, Skip Griffin, was getting ready to work with a special forces team at the Department of Defense. As he was thinking about what he wanted to talk about with this group, life conspired to connect him with a well-known general who had been instrumental in developing the whole field of counterintelligence work. This general lived in Skip's hometown, and a few days before his training session they ran into each other. Skip happened to mention the work he was about to do and described to the general this idea of readiness and his sense that it is a key attribute of highly effective teams. The general knew exactly what Skip was talking about and told him this story:

> *"I remember one morning when I was in Korea. It was a quiet morning, and all seemed normal. Walking slowly along, I began to notice very small, subtle elements in the environment around me—the color of the greenery off to one side was slightly too green, there was the slightest hint of smells like tobacco smoke and coffee. Having grown up on a farm, I learned at an early age to use all my senses to take in my surrounding. I instinctively dropped to the ground and a bullet went flying overhead precisely where I had been standing milliseconds prior. If someone has not cultivated this kind of perpetual readiness in themselves, they do not survive."*

When Skip shared this story at the Department of Defense training, the participants got the idea immediately. Special forces work requires an extreme degree of readiness. Spending months on end in wilderness environments had cultivated my own version of this capacity. When I was miles and sometimes days away from help should an emergency arise, a quiet and keen sense of awareness was vital—constantly discerning when to act and when to pause. This place of readiness kept us all safe. When the outer environment seemed clear and fine, yet inside something felt off, these were the days we stayed at base camp rather than pushing the envelope. Safety and survival were the key metrics of success. Living with these basic realities engenders a deep intelligence filled with a practical and essential wisdom. It is an alternative type of education, hard to get if our lives become too comfortable, if we don't keep our senses honed to the shifting impulses in each moment. In many respects, when we lived closer to the earth and had to engage on a daily basis with the vagaries of weather, hunting, planting, and shelter, there was no choice but to sustain a place of readiness. We couldn't afford not to, as this quote implies:

"Some of the mountain men were finely educated, some were not, but all were extremely practical men whose minds were beautifully tuned. They could not be dull, for to let their wits dull was to invite death.

"One does not need education to be intelligent, and these men might be short on what educated men use in the way of information, but their wits were sharp, their minds were alert, they were prepared to move, to change, to adapt at the slightest need. All about them were conditions and circumstances to which they must adjust, attack by Indians or outlaw trappers was an ever-present danger, they lived on

the very knife-edge of reality and when this is so, the
mind becomes a beautifully tuned instrument.

   "They did not fall into patterns or ruts. There
were none. . . ."[3]

Living on the Edge

I have seen many times how taking people into the wilderness
begins to awaken this deep intelligence. The challenge is to
keep it alive when you return to the normal circumstances of
daily living. Keys to this challenge can be seen in the quote
above: being able to move, to change, and to adapt; not falling into patterns or ruts. These two attributes can be actively
cultivated and lie at the heart of readiness and Leadership
Flow. And I believe opportunities for practice abound if you
know where to look.

    Catherine is strategic advisor and director of commu-
nications and marketing for the University of Chicago's
Laboratory School. As a member of the senior leadership
team, she was one of eight charged with leading a strategic
planning and engagement process for the school. It was a
moment in time when tensions between faculty and admin-
istration were at an all-time high and trust at an all-time low.
Creating a process to uncover current challenges and think
together about possible futures, she joined me in facilitating
a conversation with thirty faculty members. Shortly after the
session had begun, I asked people to share specific and concrete examples of current problems. A vocal and agitated
faculty member pointed directly at Catherine and said, "You
and your team are the main problem!" Silence crackling with
tension filled the room. Everyone waited. And then Catherine
began to speak. With courage, humility, and honesty she told
her own story of being a former student, and the challenges
she had faced working for five different directors in the last

six years. Like pulling the plug in a bathtub, the anger and hostility drained out of the room in response to her authenticity and openness. An honest, genuine, and heartfelt exchange occurred, a start in the long arc of building a better future together. One step.

Breaking Old Patterns

For me, Catherine's story is a beautiful example of what readiness and intelligence look like in a contemporary context of leadership. She kept her wits about her, adapted in the moment, and met the need squarely. Leaning in rather than away, she made the perfect "leadership move." Breaking the pattern of "us versus them," she opened the door to explore the intertwined humanity of Lab School as a community. It took tremendous strength to stay in the room, keep breathing, and not fall into the rut of roles and structural power dynamics. Connecting with her during a short break, I found her literally shaking from the intensity of the encounter. Despite the intense discomfort of this experience, Catherine leaned into this learning edge and continued her active engagement with all stakeholder communities. Through these engagements she was able to draft an inspired and inclusive strategic framework reflecting shared ownership of the vision, outcomes and opportunities for the Lab School going forward.

Breaking out of old patterns and ruts takes guts and fortitude. Believing in yourself, you take a risk to do something totally different. Guided by the stream of intelligence flowing in from all directions, you stay present, pivot quickly, and continually adapt. This is how you keep alive the capacity of readiness—a state of relaxed awareness where new and latent possibilities lie waiting.

Explore, Engage, Experiment

The first step in building a state of readiness is to examine your current habits and routines. Look at how much of your life is filled with activities running on autopilot. Start to wonder about the unconscious "ruts" you may be falling into, dulling your experience of aliveness and ability to adapt and change. Think about the tension between action and non-action—doing things simply for the sake of not having to confront "empty space." Muse upon these questions. Start to notice moments when non-action is the best action.

- *What is my current experience of readiness?*
- *If there is one "rut" preventing me from anchoring to the moment, what would it be?*
- *How comfortable am I waiting in the place of non-action until it becomes clear what to do next?*
- *What is one shift I could make today to increase my state of relaxed awareness, my ability to be totally present?*

Out of the field of readiness comes precision—action precisely appropriate to the situation at hand. Not too big and not too small. The perfect action at the perfect moment creating change and lasting impact.

Precision

One of the most powerful examples of precision in action occurred on December 1, 1955, in Montgomery, Alabama:

> *"The city's bus ordinance didn't specifically give drivers the authority to demand a passenger to give up a seat*

to anyone, regardless of color. However, Montgomery bus drivers had adopted the custom of moving back the sign separating black and white passengers and, if necessary, asking black passengers to give up their seats to white passengers. If the black passenger protested, the bus driver had the authority to refuse service and could call the police to have them removed.

"Three of the other black passengers on the bus [that day] complied with the driver, but Rosa Parks refused and remained seated. The driver demanded, "Why don't you stand up?" to which Parks replied, "I don't think I should have to stand up." The driver called the police and had her arrested."[4]

Rosa Parks had ridden this bus for years, but on this particular day she chose a totally new and different action. The outer action she took was very simple—she did not stand up. The internal shift was seismic. In that moment she claimed her right as a free woman to stay in her seat. She was no longer a woman of color; she was a free woman, and as a free woman she had the right to remain seated. Inner conviction met precise and very simple outer action: sitting in a seat. The story of her being physically tired was untrue. She was tired of "giving in" to the story being told by her surroundings. The timing of the moment was perfect, and the impact was huge.

Years of Practice

It is naïve to think she simply woke up on the first of December, and voila, she decided to do something huge and dramatic. In actual fact, Parks had spent years preparing a place of readiness. An active member of the National Association for the Advancement of Colored People (NAACP) for over twenty years, she had steadily been making deep internal changes in her own perception of herself as well as engaging with others, learning, sensing possibilities, and building communities of practice. As the story goes, she did not plan to stay in her seat; it came as an impulse in the moment, and she committed to the action without hesitation. It was the precise action at the right moment and was part of her destiny. This is the power of the direction of Within. Action coming moment by moment balanced with waiting and non-action.

Caretake the Moment

Discerning real action from a seemingly perpetual barrage of possible things you could do is high leverage leadership work. Built by taking small steps over time it comes down to one simple practice eloquently described centuries ago by the Greek philosopher Epictetus:

Caretake this moment.
Immerse yourself in its particulars.
Respond to *this* person, *this* challenge, *this* deed.
Quit the evasions.
Stop giving yourself needless trouble.
It is time to really live; to fully inhabit the situation
   you happen to be in now.
You are not some disinterested bystander.
Exert yourself.
Respect your partnership with providence.
Ask yourself often, How may I perform this
   particular deed
such that it would be consistent with and
acceptable to the divine will?
Heed the answer and get to work.
When your doors are shut and your room is dark
   you are not alone.

The will of nature is within you as your natural
    genius is within.
Listen to its importunings.
Follow its directives.
As concerns the art of living, the material is your
    own life.
No great thing is created suddenly.
There must be time.
Give your best and always be kind.

Caretake the moment. As this poem reminds us, we are never alone but in partnership with providence. Precision comes when the direction of Above—greater intelligence—joins with Within—present moment. Listening and then acting with conviction, back to listening again. Choosing what to do and what *not to do*. Less action becomes right action at the right time. And the only thing you need to do is listen for the one next step and take it.

The One Next Step

Action in this way is based on taking one next step at a time. It has a sequence that is both deliberate and highly spontaneous. Take a step, notice the impact, wait for the ripple effect, and then listen for what comes next. Often there may be a series of steps, one after another with only the briefest of pauses between. On close reflection, you will be able to discern a sequence. The key question to ask when it comes to this kind of precision is "What is the *one* next step to take in this exact situation?" All action begins with discerning a first step and then taking it decisively and without hesitation.

Greg McKeown's book *Essentialism: The Disciplined Pursuit of Less* emphasizes the importance of building the "one step at a time" muscle and reveals the real downside when you don't. "The idea that we can have it all and do it all is not new. This myth has been peddled for so long, I believe that virtually everyone is infected with it . . . It is championed in corporations. It is embedded in job descriptions . . . What *is* new is how especially damaging this myth is today, in a time when choice and expectations have increased exponentially."[5] The by-product of this behavior is lots of time spent either undoing what has been started or pushing and prodding people to complete tasks that inevitably fall off the to-do list because they are not in sync with the larger momentum.

Start close in. Look directly at the habit of initiating too many things and not having the time or energy to bring them all to fruition. Rest in the moment and listen before rushing in. And when the first step appears, take it.

Explore, Engage, Experiment

Practicing the art of precision often means breaking one of two habits. Some are paralyzed because the situation seems overwhelming and any action seems risky, so they do nothing. Others leap in and simply do something in order to appear in charge, falling into the classic leadership image that they have "the answer." The practice of One Next Step is the antidote for breaking both these habits.

> Pick a current challenge you working with. See if you can identify the first step, one step that you could take, knowing that this step will, indeed, have an impact. You can then pause, notice the impact, and ponder the next step.

Often as you begin to work this way, a short sequence of steps will come in a precise order. Experiment with a short sequence. Action—pause—reflect. Repeat.

Pausing, readiness and precision are the key practices of Within. Progress becomes clear as you notice the rhythm and pace of your work and way of interacting.

Getting Traction

Living in the present moment is a combination of discipline and relaxation. At times, my husband and I make our home available for people to come and receive in-depth coaching and/or healing work offered by my husband. Last year a couple came and spent a week with us. Upon leaving, the wife had this to say, "The most remarkable experience I had this week was watching the two of you. It is totally amazing to me how much you accomplish each day with what appears to be so little effort and no sense of rushing around. It has made me really think about things differently."

The direction of Within is characterized by not rushing. The image of a well comes to mind—a perpetual spring bubbling up from inside. When we move too quickly, we stay slightly out in front of the full nourishment of our inner wellspring. Staying anchored in the present places us squarely in the middle of a spring connected directly to our sense of "well-being"—Being the Well. Non-action and right action are equally present in this place; both are of equal value and dance back and forth with each other. The organ of the heart gives us a profound clue about pace as Brother David Steindl Rast reminds us, *"The heart is a leisurely muscle. It does not get tired because there is a phase of rest built into every heartbeat."*[6] In a heart that has been beating for a hundred years, sixty-seven of those years were at rest! Contemplate the pace of your days. Notice when you are slightly out in front of the moment and come back.

Getting traction in the direction of Within is directly experienced in the pace of your day. Characterized by what my coach and horse trainer calls "No Hastings," the overall rhythm of the day is that of calmness. There is no rushing around. Pauses, however brief, abound as you discern what to do and what not to do. Ask yourself the following questions:

- *What is the current pace of my day?*
- *Do I feel nourished by the pace or depleted?*
- *What is one first step that I could take to begin to shift the overall pace and rhythm of my day?*

Chapter 6:

Below: Respect Creation

○⌇⌇⌇⌇⌇⌇⌇⌇⌇⌇⌇⌇⌇⌇⌇⌇⌇⌇⌇⌇⌇⌇⌇○

"We are here to awaken from our illusion of separateness."
                                        —THICH NAT HAHN

*D*esigned in the 1990s, the landscape and surrounding grounds of the National Museum of the American Indian (NMAI) beautifully and meticulously represent the experience and understanding of Native American peoples. Four carefully chosen stones have been placed in each of the cardinal directions: East, South, West, and North.

The youngest of the four stones is a lava ball from the Keamoku Lava Flow at Hawai'i Volcanoes National Park near Hilo. Shaped like a giant bowling ball, the stone is estimated to be between three and four hundred years old. In November of 2003, the team met with the Volcano Kupuna, a council of Native Hawaiian elders who oversee cultural activities at the park. After some discussion, the Kupuna representatives explained that stones are the body and living spirit of Pele, the volcano goddess. They believe it is taboo to remove stones from the Hawaiian Islands, and those who do so without permission face retribution from Pele.

Several months later, the team returned to Hawai'i at the request of the Kupuna, who explained that a ceremony existed to temporarily remove the stone from the Kilauea Volcano. The Kupuna selected a stone for the western marker and named it Kane Po, meaning "light and dark," during a special naming ceremony. Like many Hawaiians who travel to the mainland to study and work for a time, the rock would return home after a period of twenty years. A new stone from another island would be selected to take its place, continuing the cycle and the relationship. After the Kupuna ceremonial blessing, the four-thousand-pound stone was transported to the harbor in Hilo and shipped from Hawai'i to Oakland, California, where it was unloaded and driven across the country.[1]

Imagine a world where this level of care was brought to all aspects of creation: plant, animal, human, animate, and inanimate. This *is* the worldview represented by the direction of Below. And the practice begins with respect.

Respect

Heading back to my hotel after a long day of work in Washington, DC, I was standing at a crosswalk waiting for the light to change. Out of the corner of my eye I noticed a homeless woman coming up beside me. Unaware of her surroundings, she started to step into the street. Instinctively I put out my arm, stopping her. Stepping back abruptly, she snapped awake as a big bus sped by. A poignant interaction followed. Straightening up her posture, she smoothed her rumpled dress. "I must smell. It's been a while since I've had a bath," she stammered.

"You smell just fine," I said, which was true. Shortly thereafter, the light flashed white indicating it was safe to walk. Together we crossed the street.

At the corner, she turned and thanked me. Taking her hand in mine, I replied "My pleasure. You have a good evening and take care of yourself." Turning we went our separate ways.

Tribal by Nature

Having never lived on the streets, I cannot speak of this path. What I do know is there are growing numbers of people who find themselves homeless. On my morning commute to Regis University, I drove by a corner where there was always a homeless man or woman sitting. Noticing my discomfort as I drove by each day, I contemplated what action I might take. Research shows one deeply debilitating aspect of homelessness is the experience of isolation, of being invisible and treated as if you didn't exist. Tribal by nature, humans are hard-wired to link our sense of survival to the experience of community. Human evolution has occurred primarily in small groups, not mass societies, causing us to instinctively seek out social networks. Throughout history we have survived by the strength of our tribes and our connection and association with others.[2]

Knowing this, I chose interaction and acknowledgement as my primary action. To this day I greet and acknowledge my homeless community members whenever and wherever I encounter them. My acknowledgement almost always brings an immediate experience of connection and a reciprocal greeting. And thankfully I have friends and colleagues whose destiny is to work directly with the other complex and practical needs of this particular sector of humanity.

Reciprocity

As we are inherently tribal by nature, it's no wonder genuine community ranks so high on our scale of work satisfaction. With the increase of working from home or in cubicles where progress is evaluated by numbers of products pushed out the door, deliberately attending to community becomes important. Any business that figures this out stands out as a true model of success. The *Boston Globe* was a case in point.

When the newspaper was in its heyday, those close to CEO Bill Taylor describe his leadership as one of transparency, integrity, and employee engagement. To generate a level of loyalty deep and widespread, everyone was involved in helping to set goals for the coming year. Sometimes people would come up with overly optimistic goals, and they would need to go back and rework the numbers in order to create realistic targets. These goals were critical because they set revenue targets directly linked to bonuses.

Bill was very up front and explicit about everything—what the compensation was, bonus targets, state of play in the industry, and things to expect as well as challenges confronting the company. The biggest portion of the bonus, often around 60 percent, was based on team performance. Everyone needed to contribute for the company to succeed. And when they had a bad year, everyone took the hit including the top leadership. Black Monday in 1987 was a good example. It was a bad time in the newspaper industry, and when the company needed to cut costs, the top guys took furloughs—vacation without pay.

Bill Taylor is not alone in creating employee-centric models of leadership. Bob Chapman, bestselling author of *Everybody Matters: The Extraordinary Power of Caring for Your People Like Family,* has been developing his people-centric approach for over two decades and is part of an emerging movement called "conscious capitalism."[3]

Conscious capitalism seeks alternative approaches to business which honor all stakeholders, all employees and the planet we all share. As a movement, it points to the inherently reciprocal nature of all relationships—a dance of give-and-take. How each person is treated matters, regardless of the position they hold in the company, and is the measure of actual respect in the company as a whole. Respect, belonging, and a sense of community are essential for individuals' ability to contribute. Increase individual contributions, and the success of the company follows. In a reciprocal relationship, one act of respect builds upon another. And most often these acts are found in seemingly small everyday details.

Attention to Details

Building respect applies to all the details of our lives, from seemingly small tasks like the way you handle a chainsaw when cutting firewood to apparently larger events like the sudden loss of funding when an investor decides to pull out. *Caring for the concrete, physical realities of our lives is where we demonstrate our understanding of this direction.* What you do in private matters as much as how you show up in public. The idea of being able to "turn on and off" respect depending on the stakes of a given situation is an illusion. Often the higher the stakes, the more automatic the response. And if you haven't been handling the small moments with respect, good luck doing so with the big ones! Use all the smaller, less volatile experiences to build this muscle so when real pressure comes on, it will become your default way of acting.

Explore, Engage, Experiment

Respect is a way of acting with each detail of your life. Contemplate your current life.

- *Where or what do you find yourself running rough-shod over? A person, an activity, a physical place or situation?*
- *What would need to shift in you to begin to act with deeper respect?*

Pick one place and experiment with engaging in that situation with more attention and respect. See what happens.

Tending the Field

With each action we lay invisible lines of connection—with people, with the environment, with our animals, with the larger global community. The old adage "as you sow so shall you reap" is indeed true. If the seeds you are sowing are genuine and respectful, you can build a real relationship with virtually any aspect of creation. The key is genuinely caring and wanting to connect. Once you begin to walk in this way, all manner of possibilities will arise. Relaxation and curiosity take the place of impatience and discomfort. How will my actions ripple out into the world? What will come back along these lines being laid?

Interconnection

As I sat in a small house in the hills of Cape Town, South Africa, the living room erupted with cheers. Nelson Mandela had been elected president. After working in southern Africa since 1988 amidst the tension and constant constraints of apartheid, it felt like a dam had burst and the water of new possibilities might now flow. Caught up in the moment, I rode the wave of excitement and promised to find money to launch a new Leadership School in South Africa.

Upon returning to Colorado, the reality of needing to raise funds for my own Leadership School in the US brought me down from the clouds. The commitment to my waiting friends in South Africa began to feel overwhelming. How on earth could I find the money to get them going when I didn't have the funds for my own school? Confronted with these seemingly insurmountable challenges, I did what any smart person does—I put the situation out of mind and tried not to think about it, lest I end up totally depressed.

Not surprisingly, the call came when least expected. Focused on the details of my day, I casually answered the phone. A man with a heavy accent said, "I hear you have a project. What's the number?" For a split second, I almost hung up, as I had no idea what he meant and assumed he had reached me in error. And then, like a flash, I saw South Africa. He wanted to know how much money was needed to get the school up and running! It had only been a couple weeks since I'd arrived home, and no one had taken the time to figure out what it would truly cost.

Stumbling over my sentences, I said we didn't have the exact figures but would get back to him quickly.

Seizing the Moment

I called the team in South Africa, and they pulled together our best guess of costs for the first three years of start-up. Two short phone calls later and I was on a plane to Florida to meet with this donor. Simultaneously, Gary, the new executive director for the South African School, was flying over from Cape Town. Gary left with a check for $250,000, enough to cover the first three years of costs for the South African school. The icing on the cake was a second check for $100,000 which fully funded the Colorado school for the next year including several sorely needed items not even in the budget. Talk about the universe delivering! If I ever needed confirmation of a wisdom and intelligence operating at a vastly different scale than I could imagine, this particular experience made it crystal clear. And although it seemed to happen instantaneously, pieces of the foundation had been laid over a number of years.

A Collective Field

Friends, organizations, and like-minded professionals had been initiating small prototypes of interaction since the mid-1980s. Through my former USSR connections, we created a tri-continental leadership experience in Botswana bringing together American, Soviet, and Botswana youth. These programs served as a training ground for local South African staff and instructors. As the South African team began to come together, they in turn had all their own connections and contacts. Steadily and almost imperceptibly, a collective field of readiness was being built, each person playing their part, listening for their contribution.

Projects come to life through the momentary wisdom and intuitive action of individuals, all of whom are directly and unequivocally connected to this vast matrix of intelligence. Webs of connection are continually being activated by all of us all the time. New threads are being added, threads shifting, changing, rearranging. Although it can appear differently, *we are never alone.* I find this awareness humbling and energizing. Seen from this perspective, taking credit for anything as solely my own is extremely short-sighted. All creative endeavors spring from the "We." The only part I need to worry about is my thread. Tending to this thread inherently connects my piece to the larger web.

Explore, Engage, Experiment

Imagine your life securely imbedded in the web of creation. Holding this image as real and true ponder the following questions:

- *Where are those places in your life that you feel are islands of isolation?*
- *What would you do differently if you held the awareness that every aspect of your life is directly connected to the whole?*
- *How might you live differently?*
- *How might you lead differently?*

Whatever you choose to focus on is what grows in your life. If you want to know what is really important to you, simply look at the ways you spend your time—actually spend it, because these are the things which will grow.

Grow

Cross-country skiing with a friend, we were in a conversation about the state of the world when she said, "I know that I need to spend time reading about all the beheading by ISIS, but I just cannot bring myself to do it."

Offering an alternative view, I said, "Why choose to focus your energy in that direction? Awareness is one thing, but lots of time focusing on this will only cause it to grow— first inside yourself and then in the larger world." Forgetting this truth unintentionally adds "fuel" to things that do more harm than good. Instead, turn toward the things you want to see increase. Reclaim the power of your conscious attention. Focus it on things you want to see grow and flourish.

A Reinforcing Loop

Attention is like any precious resource. It needs to be used wisely and with intention. Operating out of unconscious habits, our lives slowly fill up with all kinds of things we didn't intend. A reinforcing loop is set in motion, and momentum gathers in whatever direction we focus on. Take the issue of work/life balance as an example. Starting small— just one more email—gradually work creeps its way into all the nooks and crannies of your life. You slowly stop noticing you have opened up your phone yet again to check for messages. Before you know it, work has taken over, leaving little space for other things. It is like going down to your vegetable garden one day and noticing it is filled with only one vegetable—kale! How come it is all kale and nothing else? Because kale is all you have been planting. If you want more variety, start planting other crops. Use your conscious attention to sow some new seeds. Variety is not only "the spice of life"; it is essential for your own health as well as the health of your garden.

Variety

Monocultures of any kind, be they activity-related or food-related, are problematic. Healthy ecosystems always include a wide variety of species. In the context of the seven directions, the word *grow* means bringing back variety and diversity, not getting rid of them. "Growing your business" is a common phrase, usually meaning making more money, adding more people, or producing more product. Of themselves, these can be fine outcomes, but the issue is *at what cost*? Agribusiness is the classic example of growing a farming business. Big swaths of land producing single crops. At the beginning outputs do go up, but over time the health and well-being of the soil goes down. As the soil becomes exhausted, more chemicals are needed to keep it productive. A reinforcing loop away from health toward depletion sets in and gathers momentum. Thinking in loops versus lines is part of taking the whole into account. Following the trail of initial actions to overall impacts on the entire ecosystem is the practice with success being measured in terms of health and well-being of people, local communities, and the planet itself.

Health of the Whole

The whole is always being considered. Separating out a part without considering the impact on everything to which it is connected is where problems arise. And typically, it is humans who separate themselves from the very ecosystems upon which their survival depends. This habit needs to be flipped on its head. In the words of the poet Wendell Berry, it requires a reorientation in how we think about what we are working on:

"We have lived our lives by the assumption that what was good for us would be good for the world. We have been wrong. We must change our lives so that it will be possible to live by the contrary assumption, that what is good for the world will be good for us. And that requires that we make the effort to know the world and learn what is good for it."[4]

Making the effort to "know the world and learn what is good for it" is the essence of Below. Creating meaningful, life-giving work in our complex and interconnected modern world is the challenge.

Models for the Future

Experimentation with these ideas is definitely happening. The fair-trade movement is one example. The benefit corporation movement might well be another. Like conscious capitalism, benefit corporations are a new form of incorporation where the company is required to balance purpose and profit with well-being and sustainability. Legally required to consider the impact of their decisions on their workers, customers, suppliers, community, and the environment, they must meet specific, measurable metrics balancing profitability with long-term, generational sustainability. The assessment process is rigorous and requires clear, undisputable data to back up espoused principles and practices. As a result, only a small percentage of the organizations taking the assessment have enough direct action on the ground to become a certified benefit corporation. For those organizations certified and practicing the integration of profitability and sustainability, their return on investment stands up to their peers and in some cases surpasses them.[4]

The search is on for new models, and these movements hold seeds of possibility. Perhaps they can provide a springboard for your own inquiry and explorations.

Explore, Engage, Experiment

Take an inventory of the "garden of your life." Think specifically about all aspects of your life at this moment including family, friends, community, work, play, time for self, and so on. With the image of a garden as the guiding metaphor, ask yourself the following questions:

- *How does your garden grow?*
- *Are most of the plants healthy?*
- *Do some need more attention?*
- *Is there a good variety?*
- *Is there a particular plant that you really love that is not currently planted?*
- *What would you need to do to plant even a small amount of this plant?*

Contemplate these questions and one next step that you could take to somehow enhance the garden of your life.

I invite you to get to know the world in all its myriad forms. Step outside your door and notice the vast array of opportunities awaiting. Pick one and begin.

Getting Traction

When the pace of living—as was outlined in Within—becomes more natural, diversity starts appearing in seemingly mundane circumstances. It is everywhere—the changing weather of each moment, the turning leaves on a tree, the quiet opening of a flower. Everywhere. Interacting with the range of people, plants, animals and events coming naturally your way and noticing the rich and wide diversity of life are sure signs you are opening the direction of Below.

For the next week start looking at your immediate world at work and at home through the lens of variety—appreciating the variety, looking for it, seeing it, and honoring it. At the end of the week, write three pages in your journal of what you noticed as you practice the direction of Below.

Over time if you see more richness and variety in your life, you can be sure you are getting traction in this direction.

Upright and Rooted

Connecting with the deep flow of wisdom, staying present, and rooting our actions in the earth—Above, Within, and Below—these are the three directions comprising the vertical axis of being. With these three in place, we can learn to dance and move with the steady winds of change that make up the horizontal axis of action.

PART THREE:

Dancing with the Winds of Change

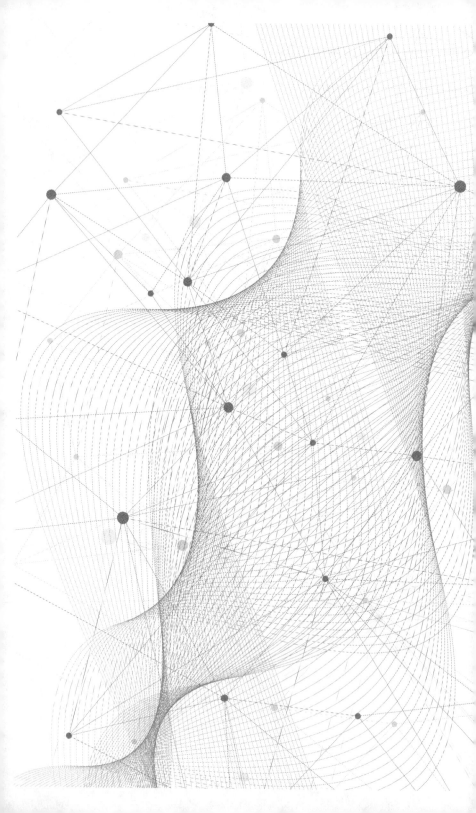

Chapter 7:

Leadership Flow in Action

"Talent is cheaper than table salt. What separates the talented individual from the successful one is a lot of hard work."

—Stephen King

In the late 1980s, a miniature version of the planet was constructed to study plants and living systems. Known as Biosphere 2, it was a totally indoor ecosystem. Many interesting things were learned, and perhaps of most note was the role of "wind." Although the trees planted grew faster than they would have in the wild, what they didn't do was survive. Never completely maturing, they would collapse. As it turns out, this was because they had no interaction with the wind.

In the wild, the wind constantly keeps them moving. This movement creates stress that, in turn, causes the trees to grow something called "reaction wood." This wood has a different structure, allowing trees to sway and grow in all kinds of contorted shapes optimal for their survival. The same dynamic holds for plants. Plants grown solely indoors tend to be weaker than when they become exposed to the elements. Their structures are strengthened by the "stress" caused by wind.[1]

Without the wind, trees cannot grow and be strong. And so it is also true for humans. We need the "stress" of change and uncertainty to grow, learn, and thrive. Too much comfort, living in an overly controlled environment weakens the human operating system in much the same way it does trees and plants. For our own health and ability to survive, we must learn to dance with the winds of change. Understanding the four directions making up the horizontal axis of doing is how we learn to do this dance.

Our Personal Vehicles

Arriving in Pittsburgh to facilitate a National Academy of Sciences dialogue training for scientists and engineers, I was checking into my bed and breakfast. "Are you registering a vehicle during your stay?" queried the receptionist. "Only the one standing right here in front of you" I replied. As she looked up from her computer, a big smile crossed her face and she laughed. "That's good!"

Our bodies are the one highly sophisticated and customized vehicle we are given at birth and use to navigate life on earth. Ironically, unlike typical automobiles, most of us are never really given driving lessons and as a result tend to forget how to use these vehicles effectively and responsibly. Remembering how to use and care for the refined and extraordinary nature of these vehicles is the work of the next four directions.

Imagine your body as the place where "inner meets outer"—where the invisible impulses from the universe connect directly to the world of form and creation. Twenty-four hours a day huge amounts of information are coursing through your cells, setting off all kinds of physical, emotional, and mental reactions. Managing this information flow and turning it into wise and creative action is the lifelong art of learning how to "drive" your personal vehicle while you are here on Planet Earth.

A good place to start is remembering a couple "rules of the road." Somewhere between the ages of eighteen and twenty, you are meant to begin being a responsible driver. For the next decade, imagine you have your "learner's permit." By the time you hit thirty, the driver's seat is yours.

Back in the Driver's Seat

Jane, a budding entrepreneur, is a perfect example of this first rule of the road. A petite and lively woman, she dropped heavily into a chair at the opening of a four-day leadership training program. Thoughts spinning, sentences incomplete, she was scattered and stressed. The clarity and focus needed to manage all the moving parts of her life were totally out of reach. Operating at breakneck speed, she had no time to stop, pause, or reflect on what she was doing, let alone choose the appropriate action. With a few days of time and space away from the normal fray of her life, she began recalibrating and finding her footing again. By day four, Jane had found her way back to herself. Her closing reflection was this:

"Coming into the room, I felt like a flag flapping wildly on the side of a locomotive barreling down the tracks. The last four days I've been tumbling toward the engine, and this morning I landed up in the driver's seat again . . . The train is still hurtling down the tracks, but at least I'm back where I belong and can gradually take over running this thing called my life!"

Landing back in the "driver's seat of your life" is the primary aim of the Axis of Doing. Once you are in the driver's seat, you can start using your vehicle with ever greater consciousness: noticing your speed, changing gears deliberately, and navigating smoothly through and around the daily realities of living.

Four Interrelated Capacities

Continuing this analogy, there are four basic "gears" or capacities represented by the four directions and the skills they embody: *East: Become Emotionally Agile, South: Build Physical Resilience, West: Cultivate Mental Fluidity, and North: Embrace your Spiritual Destiny.* Each of these directions has a slightly different set of functions. With mastery they allow your daily living and leadership to be filled with integrity, dignity, precision, and authenticity.

These four capacities dynamically dance with each other. For example, every thought going through your mind is accompanied by a feeling and vice versa. Noticing the interconnection between thoughts and feelings, you have two different angles of exploration when a situation appears in which you feel "stuck." Similarly, an effective way to quiet a "spinning mind" is to get physical and go for a walk. Walking tends to quiet the mind, letting a deeper flow of new insight come through. Imagine you now have four different angles from which to generate new perspectives other than simply sitting at your desk trying to force some kind of insight. Instead, get up and move. Get outside, give the challenge to the universe, and let your mind relax. Do something that engages your heart. Pick something you love to do. Activities we love are hard-wired to our spiritual DNA. Body, mind, heart, and spirit work together to keep you connected and on track. All guided by what you could call your "cosmic operating system"—the vertical Axis of Being—where driver and destiny dance together to arrive on time at destinations designed by the intelligence of life. With the Axis of Being as your internal guidance system, you can embrace these next four capacities and learn how to use them with accuracy and precision. Patience, compassion, and curiosity will be your constant companions as you lean into each direction and find new habits of action. We begin in the direction of the East: the Heart.

Chapter 8:

East: Become Emotionally Agile

○∞∞∞∞∞∞∞∞∞∞∞∞∞∞∞∞∞∞∞∞○

If we lack emotional intelligence, whenever stress rises, the human brain switches to autopilot and has an inherent tendency to do more of the same, only harder. Which, more often than not, is precisely the wrong approach in today's world.

—ROBERT K. COOPER, BESTSELLING AUTHOR AND
CEO OF COOPER STRATEGIC

*B*y the age of three, I was a skilled temper-tantrum thrower. My mother was totally unflappable. No matter what I did, I couldn't get a rise out of her, and it drove me nuts. I'd hurl myself down on the carpet in front of her and let loose with the screaming. Quietly and without fanfare, she'd get up, walk into the next room, and sit down again. Tantrums are no fun without an audience, so I'd stop, pick myself up, stomp into the next room, and begin to cry and scream again.

The ability to turn my tantrums on and off was an early

clue that, although my robust emotions were connected to me, they were also slightly separate. As toddlers we begin to learn this lesson. As leaders we often forget and then reap the consequences, getting metaphorically "slapped in the face" when we try to pretend feelings do not matter.

Our emotions are real and powerful but do not have to consume us. We have the capacity to both feel and observe ourselves feeling. This is important because an emotion observed can convert to an emotion understood. Emotions are not ends in themselves. Emotions, by design, grab and direct our attention. When we heed what an emotion is telling us, we uncover essential truths about ourselves and our world, and become more authentic beings.

Embracing emotion and moving toward it to understand its underlying message is the key practice of the East: the Heart. Operating from this perspective, you'll be careful not to make any big decisions or express hasty reactions if you are feeling unexpectedly and intensely angry or sad. You begin by pausing, noticing, and knowing you will not connect well with others or think clearly until you understand the meaning of the feeling. Exerting this self-aware control while feeling and not squelching the emotion is what is meant by "emotional agility."

Foundation of Belonging

Emotional agility allows those around you to feel safe and experience a sense of belonging. Being aware of your emotional state and having the ability to control your response creates a sense of relaxation in others. They know your choices and decisions are not coming out of a place of anxiety or fear. Google spent more than a year studying successful and unsuccessful teams, and found leaders and members of successful teams were direct, straightforward, and "sensitive to one another's moods." An unsuccessful leader exhibits, as one engineer described it, "poor emotional control. . . . He panics over small issues and keeps trying to grab control. I would hate to be driving with him . . . because he would keep trying to grab the steering wheel and crash the car."[1]

The deep intelligence of our hearts also leads us directly to our common humanity. The demonstrations during the building of the Dakota Access Pipeline in 2016, near the Lakota Sioux Standing Rock Indian Reservation in western North Dakota, provide a powerful recent example. The emotionally agile Lakota people prayed for the water and for forgiveness rather than becoming mired in anger and vitriol against the corporations that planned to place an oil pipeline underneath the Missouri River, a half mile from the reservation. The Lakota honored, with reverence, their emotional connection to the natural world. The focus was love, respect, and forgiveness.

People responded in droves. Thousands of people from hundreds of indigenous nations—as well as supporters from every state in the United States and from countries as far-flung as Tibet, Sweden, Guatemala, and Brazil—trekked to North Dakota in the dead of winter to join the peaceful gathering. Between three and four thousand people attended on any given day. Four thousand veterans came to Standing Rock to publicly apologize for the US Army's genocide of indigenous people.[2, 3]

Although fear can cause divisiveness and fragmentation, emotional agility can allow us to be drawn together across all boundaries of age, race, religion, politics, and geography in service to the greater good of the whole. Understanding this truth and knowing the importance of keeping our hearts open is key. Owning our emotions and using them to speak and act authentically, we create an environment where the whole range of unexamined emotions can be raised and explored, leading to insight, truth, and belonging.

The territory of the heart is built by engaging the four primary emotions: sadness, anger, fear, and joy. The first three of these emotions are covered in this chapter. Joy is picked up later in Chapter 11. Beginning with sadness, the capacity for deep empathy and connection, we'll explore some key essences of how the heart works.

Sadness: Connection

On a beautiful summer day in Vermont, my younger sister and I were playing in the backyard. Calling out from the porch, Mom urged us into the car so we could get to our grandmother's by midday. A visit with Nano, as we called her, was always a bit edgy. She was a force to be reckoned with, and Mom was no pushover either. Nano was very direct and sharp with her words, whereas my mother was more tactful and restrained. When a difference of opinion arose, which was often, the flow of conversation would end abruptly.

Arriving in time for lunch, we gathered around the weathered picnic table that took up much of my grandmother's small kitchen. As we chewed our ham sandwiches, the conversation seemed to be ticking along just fine as Mom and Nano talked about the weather and how the garden was doing. Shortly thereafter, the light tone of their conversation shifted. An oppressive, dark cloud—the kind that rolls in prior to a heavy thunderstorm—sucked the air out of the room. Gripped with a sudden sadness, my heart began hurting. Setting down my sandwich, I focused my gaze out the window searching for relief, for some way out of this tiny space. Big salty tears began rolling down my cheeks.

"What's the matter?" Mom asked.

"There's so much tension in this room. I can't stand it. Someone needs to let it out, and if you two won't do anything I guess it's up to me."

A moment of silence. Tilting her head toward the door, Mom and Nano got up from the table and went outside. The heaviness and heartache went with them. My sister and I were chatting and laughing when they returned.

Name the Feeling

Although we never talked about the incident further, its impact stayed with me for life. Only ten at the time, I'd had my first experience of naming an emotion and bringing it directly into the room. Naming the feeling is the first step of emotional agility, and this goes for all emotions. In order to take this first step, you need to let yourself *actually feel things*, which is not as easy as it sounds. Our modern culture often teaches us to unconsciously shut down our feelings in order to be polite or not make others uncomfortable. Turning the spigot of emotion back on can sometimes take time. Fear not, your heart is there waiting for you whenever you decide you are ready to listen. Hopefully as you walk through this chapter, some starting points for practice will become clear. Understanding a few of the key gifts and attributes of the primary emotions can be one place to begin.

Emotions as Gateways

So, what are the gifts of sadness versus anger or fear, for instance? Sadness, at its core, is about connection: with ourselves, with another, or with a wider situation. In the story of my grandmother, the sadness arose in response to a breakdown of love and respect between her and my mom. Tears signaled a loss of connection and the need to work on some kind of repair. Sadness can also surface in moments of spontaneity or beauty—a brilliant sunrise or a powerful story of love and transformation. Moments that take your breath away and fill you with a sudden and unanticipated experience of your larger surroundings. The first flush of feeling can be tears and an emotion akin to sadness. Leaning into this sensation, you go through a "gateway" and pass over a kind of threshold where the emotion shifts in intensity, and relaxation, clarity, and authentic engagement occur.

All emotions are gateways to genuine engagement and interaction. Through them we build bridges of affinity, inclusion, and belonging. Learning to discriminate among various emotions and gather the seeds of wisdom they hold takes time. And sometimes it takes unlearning old habits. For example, discerning the difference between sadness and anger. Given the current cultural norms of masculinity, when men are sad they often have learned to translate this feeling as anger because anger is more acceptable than tears. The situation is the reverse for women; when women are angry they have been raised to translate anger as sadness because getting angry was not something young girls were supposed to do. Reflect on your tendencies and see if you can identify the true, underlying emotion. To help with this discernment, we'll start with understanding sadness and then move on to anger.

Connection with Others

On a coaching call with Christine, she brought up a worrisome pattern emerging where she and her boss weren't connecting. Christine was brought into her company to pull together a global team.

Her challenge, however, was applying her people skills and sensitivity in a tough corporate culture. Attempts to ask questions, give feedback, or include coworkers in the decision-making and planning processes were being be misinterpreted by her boss. Instead of being helpful, these actions were seen as disruption or contrariness—the very opposite of Christine's intention. Over time, this dynamic was creating deep stress and fatigue.

At the start of a coaching session, Christine described how this exact dynamic had played out at a recent staff meeting. Fresh from the emotional intensity of this meeting, Christine could easily identify a feeling of sadness and name her desire for a more genuine connection. The main thing she wanted was for her boss to know ". . . that she can count on me. That I have her back." Together we created a simple structure for a follow-up conversation with her boss. It included four elements:

○ *the concrete details of what happened at the meeting*
○ *her personal feelings about it*
○ *the main story she was telling herself about the situation*
○ *what she wanted from her boss.*

With the feeling named and a clear structure for starting the conversation, she set up a meeting with her boss. Critical to the process was owning everything she was saying as what was true for her—her story, her experience—without assuming her boss was carrying the same thoughts and feelings. She left the door wide open to understand what might be true for her boss. As the conversation unfolded, up came Christine's sadness and tears. Staying steady with the intensity of emotion rising, she walked through the doorway and felt the sadness while staying engaged in the conversation. Much to her surprise, her boss had already noticed Christine's stress and unhappiness, and she was concerned too.

Connection with Ourselves

Christine's courage to open a potentially uncomfortable conversation and her boss's willingness to engage initiated a new level of trust and honesty between them—no small feat in those organizational cultures moving at breakneck speed with little time to sit and connect on a more personal level. The process also caused a deeper set of questions to surface:

How connected am I to me?
Where does my own joy fit into this equation?
How can I be myself and bring my gifts?

Questions like these are not unique to Christine; they are common in the direction of the heart. Our concerns and issues with others are often deeply and directly connected to questions about ourselves and our own choices. Honest exploration of these questions requires tremendous courage. The messages ultimately heard may well lead to fundamental changes in your work and professional direction. Directional clues about how you are using your time, energy, and gifts are almost always embedded in this emotional territory. Although we want to make it about the shifts needed in others, most of the time our hearts are pointing to shifts needed in ourselves. Such was the case with Christine, and she is not alone.

Full Circle of Trust

Connecting with the emotion of sadness and acting on insights gleaned links right back to the direction of Above—trust in life. Your emotional intelligence is embedded in the larger intelligence in the universe. *Trusting in life, you begin trusting in the wisdom of your emotions.* It is a reinforcing loop that gives you the courage to be truly yourself and in consequence allows others to show up authentically as well.

Explore, Engage, Experiment

The next time the feeling of sadness arises practice the following sequence of steps:

1. Acknowledge the presence of the feeling. If you can't explore it when or where you are, make a mental note about what's happening and commit to going back to reflect on it later. A simple way to acknowledge the feeling and commit to exploring it later is to put your hand on your heart and remind yourself—"no big deal, no drama." This physical act will serve as a memory holder for the emotion. When you find a time to reflect, you can put your hand on your heart, recall the situation, and the emotion will resurface for you to explore. (Remember that it may initially feel like anger or actually be anger.)

2. Ask yourself, *"If my heart were trying to give me a piece of advice or wisdom, what would it say?"*

3. Jot down the first intuitive, short phrase that comes to mind. Often a real piece of wisdom will surface, something you can use to take a new action or next step.

4. Embrace the wisdom you have received and find one simple, concrete action you could take.

In fairly short order, your heart will realize you are indeed beginning to listen to it, and it will speak much more often and with ever greater clarity as a result.

Connection is the outcome of embracing the emotion of sadness. Anger has its own unique language and it is the language of truth.

Anger: Truth

Anger gives us clarity. Rising with varying degrees of intensity, it signals an unseen truth about something, someone, or ourselves. Exploring it means taking a closer look because there is something we're not fully facing. It might be a deeper emotion; it might be an external situation. Examining anger's roots means asking two key questions:

Where is a boundary being crossed—
either by me or someone else?
Where am I not being fully honest?

Anger is a tireless teacher: it sticks around until all its truths are revealed. Like sadness, the raw emotion is a gateway—once we meet the energy and understand the truth it is working so hard to expose, poof! It vanishes. Yet anger asks a lot of its students. The path from anger to cause is not always straightforward. Anger might steer us intellectually to one reason ("I am furious that my partner called our client without honoring our agreement that I was the contact"), when, although there are certainly objective reasons such an action might be bad for business, "fury" is an overreaction suggesting a more significant concern. Unspoken worries about shared responsibilities, or client retention, or even mistrust about business finances or fairness can trigger unconscious associations, and our hearts make very quick leaps our minds don't always perceive. If the relationship were on solid ground, one conversation could remedy the situation.

Uncovering anger's origins can't happen when we're engulfed with emotion. The practice is staying with the emotion and pausing before going to full-blown destructive action. The more intense the emotion, the more likely the triggering event is something needing a good, close look, a new choice to be made, a different course of action than the one usually taken. With all emotions, imagine your heart is a metal detector. If there is no real "gold" in the emotion, the meter reading will register a low frequency. If, however, there is a real nugget in the feeling, the meter reading will be very high —the more gold, the louder the signal.

Understanding anger is not easy, but it is worth the effort. In its wake, anger resolved keeps you on track with your essential purpose, allowing you make clear and accurate choices congruent with your unique gifts, unclouded by misunderstandings or hidden truths.

Reframing Shadow

Figuring out anger's origins is a lifelong challenge, but you might find a shortcut through a basic understanding of what Carl Jung called "the shadow," or what some call "the shadow self." Jung's theory is that the personality traits angering us most in other people are the same traits we dislike in ourselves and have been unwilling to admit live in us too. Some of these traits are seen as negative, or even our "dark sides," such as laziness or self-importance or timidity. Others might scare us with their power and beauty. In fact, none of our qualities are either negative or positive; they are simply aspects of what it means to be human. Reclaiming any trait gives us access to more of our inherent wholeness and lets us connect with the wholeness of others.

As a faculty member for Dialogos's ten-month Leadership for Collective Intelligence program, I help participants develop emotional agility. During the morning session of a recent program, an acclaimed and well-recognized guest speaker took the group through a series of activities. He listed the steps for each activity on a PowerPoint slide show and read from the slides. Leaving little room for disagreement or discussion, he ran through his ideas as though they were the only way to think about his field of expertise. I could tell that several participants were agitated, so a few hours after he left, I opened the afternoon session by introducing the concept of shadow. As I was describing how we are often disturbed by others when they exhibit traits we dislike in ourselves, a participant named Norbert angrily interrupted me: "So are you saying that because I experienced the guest speaker this morning as a completely arrogant and self-centered b-----d, that I am really talking about myself?"

A significant pause ensued, after which I looked up and said, "Yes, that is exactly what I am saying."

A second, long pause ensued, followed by a simple response: "I guess I will have to think about that." And to his credit, he did. He thought about it, and recognized he, too, had often been called arrogant and he wasn't proud of this aspect of his personality. Naming the issue, his anger with the speaker was replaced with understanding. And together we took the important next step—we looked at Norbert's shadow without judgment. Arrogance without condemnation of others becomes confidence in one's knowledge and expertise. Diffusing the anger opens the path to productive self-exploration and the willingness to have your views questioned by others.

If the same kind of person or the same kind of action consistently makes your blood boil, take a closer look at yourself. Open yourself up to the idea, for better or worse, that you may be projecting a trait you don't want to own onto someone else. Investigate your own shadow. Can you understand the origin of the trait? Can you accept it and reframe it? Is your own timidity, for example, derived from a naturally cautious nature that enables you to accurately assess a situation before jumping in?

We ignore or try to deny our shadow self at great cost. Our shadows are parts of us, pieces we must work to reclaim.

Direct Projection

Anger typically bursts into our awareness as outwardly focused: we're mad "at" someone or something. In truth, the anger is ours alone; no situations objectively and universally prompt anger. People react to even the most overtly unjust or cruel actions in different ways: some feel sad, some feel angry, and some feel compelled to act. Owning your anger lets you use its presence as rocket fuel for deep insights, rapid shifts of behavior, and getting yourself unstuck and able to constructively respond to the situation, whatever it is.

Years ago, I ran a rapidly expanding wilderness-based leadership school. We were simultaneously developing new schools in several parts of the world. Bouncing back and forth between various corners of the globe and our home base in Colorado, I was becoming discombobulated and at times totally disoriented; once I found myself having to ask strangers on the street what country I was in and what day it was! You would think I would have gotten the message something needed to adjust, but I was young and strong, and "forward" was the one gear I knew how to operate.

I found myself increasingly irritated with one of the people working for me in Colorado. When we were both in the office, I was sure she wasn't pulling her weight. It seemed to me whenever I needed her, she was nowhere to be found. Deciding to confront her in preparation for letting her go, I called her into my office and launched into my observations.

When I stopped, she looked straight at me and said, "Don't dump your workaholic issues on me. I'm not going to work eighty hours a week and compromise my health and my life. If you want to do that, fine, but I won't."

Blam! Right between the eyes went her comment, and I was speechless. I thought I was angry "at" Nancy, and if I could get her to act differently, my anger would go away. My anger did vanish, but Nancy didn't change at all. Nancy had gotten it exactly right. I totally resented the fact she had a life outside of work and I didn't. As soon as she said her piece, my anger vanished, replaced with a strong desire to better understand my own life and habits as well as to accurately assess Nancy's work. I thanked Nancy for her comments and said that would be all, and she walked out of my office.

Over the next week I stepped back and observed her work more attentively. It turned out she was doing very good work, coming and going exactly on time, and contributing above and beyond the scope of the tasks required by her position. The only thing she was not doing was running herself ragged in the process.

This interaction with Nancy was a turning point in my awareness of the critical importance of emotional agility. If Nancy hadn't had the courage to speak up, I might not have owned my anger. I would have lost a great employee and friend and perhaps continued to work in inefficient and soul-destroying ways, which would not have helped the company in the end. After that conversation, I made some concrete shifts in my work habits and began to find a better balance between my work and life, at no detriment to the company's growth.

The gifts of anger range from deeply personal to more systemic and everything in between.

A Collective Call to Action

Sometimes anger, either within us or within members of teams we manage, reveals a situation that must be changed within the team's personnel, actions, or roles. Understanding anger as a catalyst for positive action is one of the most effective ways to increase performance, when combined with a deep respect and care for others when recommending or implementing change.

Although some people disguise their anger well, most of us wear it openly. When Tom, then the chief of the US Forest Service, heard the results of a survey of a thousand of his employees, his jaw clenched and his face reddened. All ten of us, sitting in chairs arranged in a circle, could easily see his anger, and we understood it: the report revealed an unexpected, organization-wide lack of appetite for combatting the agency's lack of diversity and inclusion.

When the team members sharing the results stopped talking, Tom was silent. For a few minutes, he stared at the papers in his lap and said nothing. When he finally spoke, his voice was edgy, his sentences short and clipped. "This is unbelievable. I cannot believe this is true. If this is really what people in this agency believe, then we have a problem. A real problem—much bigger than I imagined." He was furious.

It was clear Tom's anger was with the situation at hand and all the implications, not from an unexplored shadow or past association. Yet he did not have to react with anger. There was more to explore. As lead consultant on the project, I spoke up. I said, "Over these past few years I've seen how you work, and when you start to get angry it's a good sign. It means you're going to do something about this."

A very slight smile crossed his face. He knew I was telling the truth, and his anger was a signal to act. "When you see something you don't like, you get very cranky, and then you take a deep breath, roll up your sleeves, and figure out what to do about it. That's simply how you work."

The very next day, he called this same group together again and got to work creating a path forward. He recognized his anger was a healthy momentary response signaling a situation in need of change—tempered, as it was, by self-control. His flash of anger was a combination of disappointment in the current state of affairs and in the level of systemic changes needed which would require much more personal involvement than he had planned. But in this instance, where the cause was so clearly connected to the reaction, Tom's anger was most of all a call to act.

A Signal to Heed

Anger can signify the need for change in some very serious situations, such as perceived interpersonal or systemic abuse. The solution always begins internally. Anger tethers you to the person with whom you're angry and freezes your ability to know how to act. First examine your own reaction; for example, is your anger derived from fear and lack of control? Then listen. The insights you will eventually discover—and it can take time—about what triggered anger *within yourself* will free you to hear potential courses of action: to report your experience of abuse, to leave a job, or to step out of a ranting teenager's room.

Explore, Engage, Experiment

Anger can be momentary or persistent—its intensity is the key to determining what has caused it and what to do about it. Much of the time anger arises when life brings us a situation we don't like and we want things to be different: your flight just got canceled, someone steps in front of you to get coffee, your business proposal gets rejected. *For all these situations, breathe. Take three breaths.* Three more or ten more. Breathe, let go, relax, and then begin to consider options.

For situations where you notice you have been here before, here are a few beginning options.

- *Acknowledge the emotion and remind yourself the key, the first shift is inside yourself, not "out there." Shift, if you can, away from the emotion itself and into the role of the quiet observer. This is the place where you can have a "conversation" with the emotion itself. Ask (in a journal if you like):*

  ○ *What specifically about the situation or person makes me the angriest? Can I name it?*
  ○ *How is my anger serving me? Try to tease out a deeper insight.*
    – *Am I using this anger against myself? Am I overworking, overeating, withdrawing from others? Do I beat myself up for not being good enough?*
    – *Am I using this anger against others? Do I judge, blame, criticize, check out, overcompensate, withhold?*
    – *What would I have to let go of in order to see this person or this situation in a new light?*
    – *What is the payoff for not seeing this situation differently?*

See if you can find a starting point where the anger shifts and a small insight shows itself. At the start, reclaiming these pieces of ourselves feels forced and awkward—like learning to ride a bike. The more you practice, the easier it becomes. Reassure yourself: "There is a piece of gold in this energy for me to *mine* and *claim*. The stronger the feeling, the bigger the nugget."

Underlying Assumptions

Asking questions and becoming curious are keys to emotional agility. Engage your unexamined assumptions and notice the speed with which you jump to conclusions. Could you be lacking information about the situation or person? For example, think of a colleague who continually writes excessively long emails. You might experience this habit as "thoughtless" or "condescending" and feel angry. If you feel intensely angry, your assumption might be that your colleague doesn't care about you or even that your colleague is deliberately trying to waste your time. Now picture this: you have just been told your colleague is on the autism spectrum, and his ASD interferes with his ability to understand social cues or to succinctly express his thoughts. Where does your anger go? What is it replaced with? A deeper truth about the situation and the person. Clarity and understanding. An ally in your quest for wholeness.

Befriend your anger. Befriend your sadness. Befriend your fear.

Fear: Risk

All emotions are guides for keeping us on track; they simply operate in slightly different ways. Embracing fear and learning the wisdom of its gifts is no exception. Every major endeavor I've undertaken, whether personal or professional, involved conversing directly with fear and questions of risk. If you find yourself in a dance with fear, there's a real chance you're asking the right questions and connecting more deeply to your spiritual destiny. There's also a real chance *some kind of change* will be required, either an inner repositioning of how you understand the situation or an outer shift of lifestyle and focus.

Michele was at the top of her career as a producer for Disney Theatrical. Traveling was her way of life, from closing *Peter and the Starcatcher* in California, to Las Vegas for a rehearsal of a new cast of *The Lion King*, and then on to Chicago for the opening of *Mary Poppins* on tour. She loved her work. "When I walked into the back of the theatre and saw Bert, the chimney sweep, tap dancing across the proscenium, I started to cry. I couldn't believe how fortunate I was. I thought to myself, *It doesn't get better than this.*" The problem was after fourteen years of this intense pace, her body decided it had had enough.

In the theatre, it's normal to be extremely busy for a stretch of time, followed by pauses. After the successful opening of *Mary Poppins*, she found herself in a moment of pause. Instead of enjoying the down time, she experienced an intense and debilitating cycle of vertigo, which persisted for months. Something had to give. The big issue was her whole life—her entire sense of self—was the theatre. It was all she had ever known and done. The thought of leaving it behind was terrifying. However, she also knew her health was in serious jeopardy. Caught between two scenarios, both of which were equally scary, she took the leap and left Disney.

Taking the Risk

If the loss of her role as a theatre professional were not scary enough, the rest of her world unraveled as well. When her long-standing personal relationship started to wobble, an even deeper level of fear showed up. Right around this time, I happened to be in the neighborhood and stopped by for lunch. Sitting on the porch of the beautiful home she and her partner had built and which was now up for sale, she described the mind-numbing and paralyzing emotions engulfing her. In those quiet moments, sitting with a friend, she named the fear making her feel frozen: *could she really handle losing it all, shedding everything known in an outer sense—her job, her relationship, her home, her identity as a theatre professional?* After naming these fears out loud with a friend as witness, a real "aha!" moment occurred. If becoming totally vulnerable was the only path back to herself—the authentic Michele—then so be it. It was worth the shedding of all outer trappings. She got the answer she'd been waiting for. Yes, she could handle these risks. Fear of loss became clarity of intention.

Engaging with the emotion of fear and the risks of losing all that was familiar—the roles, the relationship, the external attachments—propelled Michele into a direct and intimate experience of herself. Summoning real courage, she walked into her fear and began reclaiming parts of herself she'd lost, parts essential for her new creative endeavors.

Archetypal Journey

Her story is archetypal. It's the heroine's journey toward wholeness, where she must meet her greatest fears to find her way back to her deepest joy. We're all on some version of this journey. Life beckons us to engage with real and direct questions about the risks of keeping our lives exactly as they are versus the risks of meeting our fears and letting things change. The practice isn't about getting a "right answer." There is no one right answer. The practice is engaging honestly with very real questions.

What am I afraid of?
Am I willing to take a look?
Can I lean into the emotion instead of wishing
it would simply disappear?
Where am I being called and why?

Situations arise all the time to give us practice in conversing with our fear and letting it give us concrete and specific
answers to all manner of life choices. More often than not,
there will be one next step to take rather than a wholesale
leap straight into the unknown. Turning toward the fear
rather than away from it is the threshold crossing experience.

Turning Toward

My dear friend Joan was having an issue with her thyroid.
Imagery scanning revealed some nodules on part of the gland.
In the absence of a definitive diagnosis, Joan was having difficulty making a clear choice about whether to have surgery
and remove the nodules or to leave them alone. Calling me,
she shared her dilemma. As I listened to her story, a simple
question arose. "Are you going to worry about the nodules
for the next six months if you don't do the surgery?"

Immediately and unequivocally she replied "Yes!" And
then she laughed out loud and said, "I guess I have my
answer!" Rather than spend six months worrying and wondering whether there was something seriously wrong, she
went ahead with what was a very simple surgery, received a
clean bill of health, and got on with living her life. The biggest
stress on Joan was her fear of the physical symptoms, not the
symptoms themselves.

So many physical ailments have fear as the deepest
stressor. Cancer is a case in point. It is often said "the diagnosis kills people faster than the disease itself." Reining in

all the imagined future scenarios and taking things one day at a time has been pivotal for friends and colleagues who have had to navigate their way through the fear the word "cancer" can engender.

Moment by moment. Not running out in front of what is happening right now. Meeting the challenges, embracing your fear of the unknown and seeing what the real choices may be. There will always be choices and challenges. The key is discerning which risks are worth taking and which ones are not.

Not Taking the Risk

In the introduction of this book, I mentioned celebrating my twentieth birthday in a steep, virtually uncharted range of mountains called the Neacolas. We were there for six weeks to climb and claim first ascents. Two of our party of four had already packed it up and skied out, leaving Mike and me to care for each other.

Our last week, our final ascent, we were making a second attempt on the highest and only named peak in the region, Neacola. After skiing for three days, we found our way to the back side of the peak to try a new route. Morning dawned clear as crystal. Gearing up and getting a good visual look at our chosen route, it looked doable and fairly straightforward. Chattering away, Mike could hardly contain his excitement. I, however, was having a different experience. The closer we got to the base of the climb, the deeper and more visceral my fear—terror actually. Using every technique in my book, I tried rationalizing away my fear, but it would not budge. As we tied into our rope to begin the climb, Mike turned to me and suddenly stopped in his tracks:

"What's wrong?!"

Swinging off my pack, I sat down and looked straight into his eyes. Panic and tears were written across my face.

"It's not right. Something is really off . . . that's all I can say."

Sitting down beside me, Mike went quiet. How long we sat I don't remember. A beautiful day in an amazingly beautiful place. And something felt wrong, really wrong. At some point he sighed and stood up.

"Guess we best get our skis on and head back to base camp."

That was it—end of discussion. At an outer level all looked clear to go, but inside me there was a sensation too large to ignore. Mike and I had built up a deep trust over six weeks. He honored this perception. We packed up and left.

Who knows? Perhaps we would have been fine, perhaps we would have died. The margin for error with just the two of us, no radios or way of communicating with the outside world, and no one for hundreds of miles in any direction was very, very small—too small on that sunny day to risk our lives for one final climb up an uncharted mountain in the middle of nowhere.

Listen and Discern

Fear comes in many packages, with a precise message for the moment at hand. In this situation, the message was "don't climb." For the five weeks preceding this moment, fear had surfaced repeatedly, but with momentary adjustments, it had been a threshold to cross and move forward. On this day, it was different, and the warning was loud and clear. This was a risk not worth taking. We all have had our own versions of this kind of fear too. A prescient sense of coming events, and guidance in terms of the path to be taken. As the saying goes, "There are old mountaineers and bold mountaineers, but there are no old, bold mountaineers." Being adventurous includes being wise. Like right and left hands, we need both to create practical, grounded, and thriving lives. Listening and discernment sit side by side as fear becomes our ally and our friend.

Explore, Engage, Experiment

Think of a situation in your life that you want to shift. Write a brief summary of the situation and then answer the following questions in this order:

1. What's at risk for me to let this situation shift?
2. What's at risk for me to keep everything exactly as it is?
3. What's the one thing I need to let go of in order to make a shift?
4. Is that a risk I am willing to take at this moment?

If the answer to question four is *yes*, this is the right moment to lean into your fear and make some changes. If the answer is *no*, then it's time to wait. Timing is important. If you get a sense it is time to make a shift, ask the following:

1. How could I reframe this situation to begin moving in a new direction?
2. What is the one, first step?
3. What support do I need in order to make this shift and handle the potential ripple effects from it?

Getting Traction

Living with emotional agility means allowing ourselves to experience the full range of emotions from jubilation to deep calm, stillness to intense grief or anger. The skill is in having the emotion and being able to choose what we do with it.

There are myriad options we can practice in our daily lives. Here are a few:

- *Express emotions deliberately and as fully as you are experiencing them.*
- *Notice the emotion and hold its energy inside until it changes into something different.*
- *See if there's a story connected to the emotion; explore the story, watching for shifts in feelings as you change the story.*
- *Physically engage the emotion's energy. If you feel angry, put your feet on the ground and walk with your focus on movement rather than on anger.*
- *Spending time in nature can also help. Try the following: Find a place in a natural setting where you can sit for twenty minutes. Get comfortable. Focus your awareness on the changes occurring around you—leaves rustling, clouds shifting, wind rising or falling, subtle temperature changes. After a few minutes of focusing on the outer world, turn your focus inward. Notice the shifting nature of feelings—a moment of sadness, then quiet, and then perhaps agitation. Let your awareness surf the outer and inner waves, smoothly moving back and forth between them.*

Reflect on your current ability to feel deeply. What emotions are you comfortable feeling and expressing? What emotions feel uncomfortable or foreign?

Find ways to engage the less familiar emotions and hear what they're telling you. See what happens as you befriend each one. As you do, the dance between the heart and the physical body will become ever more obvious. And so we move to the direction of the South, which represents our bodies and our physical resiliency.

Chapter 9:

South: Build Physical Resilience

○∞∞∞∞∞∞∞∞∞∞∞∞∞∞∞∞∞∞∞∞∞∞∞∞∞○

"The human body is a river of intelligence, energy, and information constantly renewing itself in every second of existence."

—DEEPAK CHOPRA

What could it hurt? The apricot Danish was irresistible. Wolfing it down, I launched into leading a daylong leadership training session. Approximately twenty minutes later, the impact of this Danish landed in every cell of my body. With sugar rushing to my brain, a "fog" began settling into my mind. Staying remotely coherent, let alone present and centered, required managing both my body and the content of the leadership training. I struggled for much of the day to come out of the fog and was exhausted by the end of the session. Lesson learned for certain. I'm much more careful about what I eat and where I am when I choose to eat it!

Built as finely tuned instruments of perception, our bodies are designed to thrive with the right care and attention. This is not breaking news. Bestselling author and researcher Tom

Rath has sold millions of books documenting the impact of eating, sleeping, and exercising on our ability to lead well. Making the connection between better decisions and daily energy levels, his advice is the following: "If you want to make a difference—not just today, but for many years to come—you need to put your health and energy ahead of all else."[1]

Being fully charged is analogous to a well-maintained car with a tank full of gas. Before accessing the deeper resources, intelligence, and sensitivity of your body, you've got to be able to get out of bed in the morning and meet the day with energy, resilience, and reserves. This is where we begin our exploration of the direction of the South.

Reserves

As a senior vice president of a large international financial services organization, Andrea's work required a lot of travel. Often when she arrived home after a long trip there was a great deal of tension between her and her spouse. No matter how hard she tried to be polite and loving, she would get irritable and angry, leading to some kind of fight. At her wits end, she brought up the situation on a coaching call. As we listened together, the repetitive pattern became obvious, and a simple question surfaced. "Do you notice the same tension after you have a good night's sleep or two and are rested?"

Pausing, she became very thoughtful. "Actually, now that you mention it, when I am rested and relaxed, things go quite smoothly." Understanding the impact of travel and the need for some time to get rested and recharged, she enlisted her husband's help. Together they created some new strategies to help Andrea "fill up her tank." And they made new agreements about when and where to have the important, personal conversations needed to keep things clear and open.

Timing is everything. Knowing when you are running on empty, when you are truly too tired to make clear choices and rational decisions is the starting point for building physical resilience. Fatigue, pure physical fatigue, equates to cutting short the normal long fuse of a reasonable human being. A short fuse means it only takes a small amount of fuel to set off a disproportionately large explosion!

Short Versus Long Fuse

Thinking about the long hours and stress levels of many people these days, it is not surprising we see record high levels of anxiety and tension, sometimes leading literally to acts of violence. Something as simple as a good night's rest has been well documented to impact physical health and resilience by boosting the immune system. What tends to be forgotten are the other impacts of good rest like concentration, social and emotional intelligence, and productivity.[2]

If much of this territory seems like basic common sense, why does it seem so difficult to actually make the care of our bodies a priority? Perhaps it is because it can be a "slippery slope" over time.

Gradual Slide to Denial

I worked for almost a decade with a gradually deteriorating hip. The level of discomfort and compromise grew steadily worse, and I came up with many mechanisms to compensate for the decreasing mobility. What I was less aware of was the huge toll chronic pain was taking on my physical reserves, leading to a serious erosion of my emotional and mental capacities. When I finally had surgery and was instantly out of pain, the level of exhaustion in my body was profound, and I could finally feel it. It took a full year to get back real, sustained strength again—to experience my body with a full tank of energy. I had no idea how short my own fuse had become until I experienced life with a long fuse again. My patience, tolerance, and capacity to hold much more significant issues and differences were exponentially larger when my own physical reserves were operating close to full.

A gradual slide to suboptimal health is common. Hearing the warning signals as early as possible can save a lot of pain, ineffectiveness, and heartache, not to mention time and money. Making it a priority for you sets the stage for being able to make it a priority for others.

Explore, Engage, Experiment

Recollect a time when you remember operating from a full reserve of energy. Use this as a starting point for assessing your current life.

- *Where are you on a scale of 1 to 10—with 1 being running on fumes and 10 being a full tank of gas?*
- *Where could you begin making adjustments so that your reserves refill?*
- *What is the first, one step you could take?*

A Culture of Resilience

An unconscious slide into habits eroding physical resilience permeates almost all work environments. With many start-up endeavors, the bad habits set in early on as people work long hours trying to "keep the boat afloat." Interrupting these habits early and replacing them with more sustainable, long-term options takes real discipline and self-awareness.

It is one thing to notice the link between caring for your own health as a way of building the health and well-being of your organization. It is another challenge altogether to see specific ways of creating a culture where physical resilience is taken seriously.

Cynthia is the co-founder and CEO of Pearl Certification, a new start-up creating "high performing, energy-efficient" certified homes. Dedicated to creating a culture of what she called "conscious leadership," Cynthia carried a vision of modeling and embedding sustainable leadership practices within the company. Yet even with this as a clear goal, she and her leadership team were already falling into the same trap of "working harder rather than working smarter." On a coaching call exploring some recent interactions where Cynthia felt irritable and impatient, the issue of her physical well-being surfaced. Regular exercise had fallen away in the press of daily business. Looking at options to address this imbalance, out of her mouth popped two short phrases, "Walking is good for me. Walking is good for the company!" Connecting the dots back to her vision of sustainable leadership practices, she realized the truth behind these simple sentences. As the CEO, modeling this kind of care for her own health and well-being makes it both acceptable and important for others in the company do likewise. Now her executive assistant schedules daily walks directly on her calendar. Sometimes these walks are for her own personal time and reflection; often they include others. She is even moving meetings from sitting to walking whenever she can as a way of expanding toward some new company practices rather than simply her own personal habit. And these walks accomplish several things at once: connecting with employees, listening, getting a change of scenery and keeping people sane and healthy.

Pace and Rhythm

Physical resilience is all about the art of conservation and deliberateness. A 2012 global study of 32,000 employees found that the traditional definition of engagement—the willingness of employees to voluntarily expend extra effort—was no longer sufficient to fuel the highest levels of performance. Willingness, it turns out, does not guarantee ability. Rediscovering the importance of pace in a work context turns out to be very high leverage. Creating "sustainably engaged" employees involved becoming very specific regarding time for renewal, focusing on one task at a time, feeling valued, and doing work that has purpose.[3]

If people are always being asked to move quickly and work at maximum capacity all day long, they will inevitably burn out. In the business model where humans are "replaceable parts," when someone burns out, you simply replace them with another body. Sustainable work cultures factor in pace, rhythm, and resilience. And pace will vary from person to person. As a leader, the pace you personally can keep all day is different from the pace your team or organization can maintain. Finding the accurate rhythm and pace for any given activity is the domain of mastery at a physical level. As a successful, high-altitude mountaineer, the main mantra I instilled in those I guided was to "pick a pace they could keep all day." Applying this idea of pace to the world of work, the question to contemplate is this:

> *Can you live and lead in a way which doesn't deplete your own resources, strength, or health?*

Obviously, there are extreme situations where speed is safety, and you need to go all out regardless of the physical toll. Sprint when you need to sprint and then return to a steady walk. If you have created resilience, then sprints are not problematic. The key is to listen and make small, steady course corrections. With a body rested and resilient, ever more subtle levels of insight and wisdom will become accessible. All manner of new information which may have eluded you before can now begin to be heard.

Listen

There is so much wisdom living in our bodies going unheeded. Messages often start small—a bit of stiffness here, some deep fatigue there, or an unexpected onset of dark emotion. Sometimes they come abruptly like hair standing up on the back of your neck. One of my most powerful coaching tools is the experience of goosebumps. Often, I'll be in the midst of a coaching session and suddenly the hair on my arms stands straight up. A direct signal my coaching client and I have hit the mother lode—the real issue needing to be unpacked and understood. Physical cues like this, along with voice tone and cadence, are key modes of perception in discerning root cause versus surface static and noise. Signals steering me toward precise coaching needs.

Each of us has a slightly different suite of perceptual tools. Let your body guide you. Learn how it seeks to get your attention. Use colleagues and friends to verify perceptions when you have an opportunity.

Reading the Room

Thirty-two senior leaders of the US Forest Service gathered for a two-day retreat. My facilitation partner Skip and I had done several hours of participant interviews in order to design a tight agenda. Listening carefully to the unfolding storylines on the first morning, both Skip and I sensed a "conversation beneath the one happening." A low-energy, sleepy sort of sensation pervaded the room. Quickly checking in at the first break, our perceptions aligned. Tossing out the planned agenda, we redirected the conversation to uncover unspoken tensions. As we continued to course correct and adapt over the two days, a series of genuine and critical questions surfaced leading to robust and active engagement. The result: new insights on work priorities and a breakthrough in how to create future agendas going forward. Specific exercises targeting their ability to listen—to themselves, each other and the team as a collective—were key. They left energized and committed.

The foundations of effective leadership lie in the ability to "read the room/read the person." Listening in what might be called "multiple octaves" at once—to what you see and hear visibly as well as what you hear and perceive "invisibly—builds your intuitive capacity and allows you to hear below the overt words to the nuances underneath. As you build this skill, it starts to become second nature which is good because often this more invisible or subtle information comes when you are not particularly looking for it or thinking about it.

Trusting Your Instincts

Sitting at my desk a few months ago, I suddenly stopped my work, got up, and went out to my horse paddock. Without thinking, I took off the black, mesh face masks the horses wear during the summer to protect their eyes and ears from biting flies. Five minutes later back at my desk, a brewing rainstorm cut loose and poured for the rest of the afternoon. Not only did this instinctive impulse keep both the fly masks and me from getting soaked and needing to dry out, but wet masks on the horses are agitating to them because of their very sensitive ears and faces.

As this muscle of deep listening increases, the gap between perception and action becomes almost nonexistent. Your body knows and compels you to move before you consciously register exactly why. This is what physical resilience looks like once you are operating with a full tank of gas. Movement, action, and instinct become trusted allies connecting you to the flow of information coming from the entire web of creation. Information critical and at times literally life-saving.

Prior to the tsunami hitting the coast of Thailand in 2004 and killing over 230,000 people, "messages" were coming from many directions. All the water normally lapping up against the shore disappeared—literally sucked out to sea in preparation for returning as a huge wave. The air was eerily still. All the animals free to move turned and rapidly headed inland to higher ground. Tuned to the nuances in their inner and outer environment, Thailand's indigenous tribe known as the sea gypsies sensed the early shifts in the air and the sea, remembered old stories of "giant waves," and headed for higher ground, most escaping unharmed.[4] Unfortunately, for the vast majority, the warning signs and signals of something seriously amiss didn't register. The muscle of incoming physical cues had gone dormant. A sad but true reality of our times where cell phones, GPS, body fitness tracking devices, and computers have become surrogates for our own deep perceptions.

Hearing again the ever-changing cues and nuances flowing to us through all our senses, including the surrounding environment, takes time, patience, and interest. Rebuilding this muscle is one of the most important aspects of reclaiming physical resilience.

Explore, Engage, Experiment

Reflect on your current relationship with your body and the way you listen to its wisdom. Ask yourself the following questions:

- *What are the ways that my body seeks to get my attention?*
- *How good am I at listening?*
- *How have I desensitized myself to these messages?*
- *How could I reestablish my relationship to this field of information?*

You have your own ways of listening and connecting to the wisdom of your body. The invitation is to grow and expand the depth and quality of these "conversations." In order to do this, you will need to inhabit your physical capacities—to embrace them and own them as deeply and personally as possible.

Inhabit

As bizarre as it sounds, fully inhabiting your body is not as straightforward as it might seem. Clearly, we are all inhabiting our bodies to some degree or we would be dead. The difference is between *partially and fully*—being on autopilot and being present and aware. Inhabiting our bodies is characterized by a consistent and ongoing awareness of our physical health and well-being. No judgment, only awareness in order to continuously listen. Receiving information and making subtle shifts and adjustments in what we eat, when and how we exercise, what we "ingest" emotionally and mentally, when to engage with a situation and when to retreat. Physical resilience is intimately connected with all six of the other directions, constantly registering "requests" from the other directions and integrating these as well as possible. Having been super active for much of my life, I am very familiar with treating my body as purely a "physical machine." I would push myself to go faster or farther, overriding rather than integrating emotional and mental signals trying to grab my attention.

Our Issues Become Our Tissues

Pounding the pavement as a way of working out my anger and frustration drove my "issues into my tissues," creating a serious case of sciatica. In debilitating hip and leg pain, I sought out a good acupuncturist and had a truly extraordinary experience. The session itself seemed totally innocuous. Nothing in particular seemed different and I thought, "Oh well, nice try." Crawling into bed that evening, however, something very unusual happened. A surge of rage—deep, seething rage—began coursing through my body. All night and into the next morning, waves of rage and anger surged. When they finally subsided, the physical sciatica disappeared as well! If I hadn't understood the intimate connection between physical health and the way undealt with emotional energies can become embedded in the cells of our bodies, I did now.

Our bodies are not machines. They are finely tuned instruments. As we fully inhabit these incredible vehicles of perception, an even more refined opportunity arises. Much more frequently than we think, the energy and information we are picking up on is not ours alone but is coming from the larger field of connection with others. With the birth of quantum physics, much exploration has been underway seeking to describe the interplay between individual atoms and the field surrounding their behavior. The idea of "an observer as separate from what they are observing" isn't true. Known as the "observer effect," the very act of observing something impacts the field.[5] And the wider field is always impacting us in the reverse. We are, indeed, one body of humanity sending and receiving information. Discerning the origin of incoming information—personal versus from the wider field—happens through a steady awareness of your own internal state. If you are experiencing your body as relaxed and at ease and suddenly it becomes disturbed and agitated, there is something happening in the wider field seeking your attention.

One Body of Humanity

Rolling out of bed first thing in the morning, I always went for a long, quiet walk before making my hour-long commute to Denver. A clear day with a light breeze blowing, I was enjoying the freshness of the air when suddenly my body began to get extremely agitated. For no apparent reason, I felt like crying or screaming. Full throttle, my emotions were coming unglued.

Looking around in all directions, I searched for a "red flag" of some kind—something obvious triggering my agitation. Nothing, however, seemed amiss or unusual. Given the intensity of the emotions surfacing, I turned toward home to process these feeling in private. As I came in the door, the phone was ringing, and a friend was telling us to turn on the TV. Up came the image of a plane flying into the World Trade Center—over and over again. Immediately I knew where the sudden emotions were coming from. My body had directly picked up on the huge, collective event unfolding on the East Coast—it was September 11, 2001.

We live with the illusion we are separate people, walking around as self-contained individuals, unencumbered by others. As the leading edge of science increasingly converges on ideas held for millennia by indigenous traditions and mystics, there exists a circuitry of profound interconnection running between all of us all the time.[6] Learning how to use this level of interconnectedness becomes very important. Much of what comes into our experience is not particularly personal, and yet often we look around for an external reason for the arising sensations. Inhabiting your body means managing and deciphering the wide range of sensations and perceptions coming your way. Acting as though this kind of connection doesn't exist only increases the possibilities you will attribute cause to an immediate situation when the root cause lies elsewhere. As the story above illustrates, rapid shifts internally when the outer environment seems to have shifted very little can be a starting point for deciphering root cause. The skill is increasing your momentary self-awareness.

The Body as a Tuning Fork

Certain fields of endeavor are already well-versed in this level of self-awareness. Animals operate almost completely on this level of interconnection. Master animal trainers know this deeply. When an owner brings their dog for training, the main work of the trainer is not the dog but the internal state of the owner and the impact this is having on the animal! While there are very real, concrete physical skills to master in terms of being clear and communicative with an animal, the most complex and tricky territory is helping people to become aware of what they are communicating unconsciously and often unintentionally—are they relaxed or uptight, anxious or agitated? All of these inner states are picked up immediately and directly by the animals. People do this too and then pretend we don't. Reclaiming the deep, immediate interconnection between all living forms gives you access to rich and valuable information.

Translating this awareness into the context of work, your

body becomes a constant tuning fork for what is happening around you. For example, assume you are aware of your internal state and are feeling relaxed and calm. You enter a room of colleagues for your next meeting and immediately notice your stomach gets tight and your breath quickens. This is specific and concrete information raising interesting questions. *Was there tension in the room before you walked in? Is the tension between your colleagues? Or is it related to you?* All you know to start with is your state before you entered the room versus being in the room right now. With this awareness, what do you do? Step number one—notice. Step number two—pause and breathe. Step number three—listen for what you might need to do to make the tension conscious to others and discussable. And the simple act of noticing, breathing, and relaxing, not doing anything particularly overt may be the best starting point until some other action becomes obvious. Each situation will require something different, but active awareness linked to a keen sense of your own inner state is the starting point.

Explore, Engage, Experiment

Take fifteen minutes and reflect on your current experience of your physical body.

- *How are you currently living in your body?*
- *What is the dominant emotional experience or story you tell yourself about your body?*
- *What is the dominant story that you tell others about your body?*
- *If you thought of your body differently—for instance as the most expensive and amazing violin money could buy—would you treat it differently, and if so, how?*

Staying Connected to Yourself

Tracking your internal state is one of the most effective tools in your toolkit for clear decision-making and effective leadership. Arriving at work tired, irritable, and cranky after a restless night's sleep sends a direct signal to your team, and they will intuitively steer clear. Thus, the dance of leadership, and the impact of physical resilience on what you can achieve on any given day. Reenergizing this direct, physical, and grounded aspect of leading is high-leverage. With diligence, practice, and steady listening, your body will share more and more information, and a world of subtle and accurate perception will begin to flow.

Getting Traction

The main metric to use in accessing your physical resilience is the level of patience and tolerance you have for unfolding situations. Finding yourself irritable or overly emotional, with small events triggering strong reactions, is a sign of less resiliency. If, on the other hand, you have a wellspring of patience and calm in the midst of outwardly stormy seas or unexpected obstacles, then chances are good your resilience is high. When resilience is high, your energy reserves are generally good and you have a nice "long fuse," as was mentioned at the beginning of this chapter.

One rather large caveat to this metric is an honest assessment of how fully you are inhabiting your body, including your heart and mind. A certain level of calm can be present if you have numbed yourself down, are not listening to your body, and your heart and head are asleep. This is a very different kind of calm and not the state being described here. My experience of these two entirely different states could be characterized by the words "black-and-white" versus "technicolor." In a numbed down state, the world seems grayer and less vivid. In the "fully charged" state described by Tom Rath, the world has vibrancy, aliveness, and a wide spectrum of color. Having lived in both states, I recognize the difference and work to cultivate the "technicolor" state rather than the "black-and-white" one. Having said this, there will be times when the world inevitably goes gray. Cycles come and go where these are the lessons we must learn. When this is the case, there is no judgment or shame. We learn our way through these experiences too. Some lessons only come through contrast, going to one extreme for a period of time before moving toward something new.

Experiment with the metric of gauging the length of your "fuse" and the quality of "color" in your days. Use this as a guide to discerning when to tackle the big challenges and also when to wait.

Think of this past week and the various situations you encountered where you felt your emotional temperature "rising." Reflect on the level of ease with which you handled the situation.

Was your emotional response in proportion to the event at hand?
- *How quickly did you find yourself feeling relaxed afterward?*
- *On a scale of 1 to 10—with 1 being a fuse that will explode with a tiny amount of spark and 10 being a really long fuse that could be extinguished easily—what was the length of your fuse?*

If your fuse is really short, tackle this issue first. Assuming you are working with a relatively long fuse, play with the

(continued on the next page)

(continued from previous page)

idea of "gray tones versus technicolor." You can use the same kind of scale to measure this:

- *On a scale of 1 to 10, with 1 being flat gray and 10 full technicolor, what is your dominant experience at the moment?*
- *Are there certain activities where bright colors show up? If so, what are these?*
- *If there are places with "gray tones," what might you do to bring more life into these situations or activities?*

Chapter 10:

West: Cultivate Mental Fluidity

⟨◦×××◦⟩

"The sky isn't the limit. The mind that sees this sky is the limit."

—BYRON KATIE, SPEAKER AND AUTHOR

Once upon a time, a traveler came across three stonecutters and asked them what they were doing. The first replied saying he was the most miserable person on earth and he had the hardest job in the world. "Every day I must move around huge stones to make a living, and I barely make enough money to buy food." The traveler gave him a coin and continued walking. The second stonecutter did not complain and focused on his work. When the traveler asked him what he was doing, the stonecutter replied "I'm earning a living by doing the best job of stonecutting in the entire county. Although the work is hard, I'm satisfied with what I do and I earn enough to feed my family." The traveler praised him, gave him a coin and went on. When the traveler met the third stonecutter, he noticed that the stonecutter had sweat and dust on him but he looked happy and was singing a cheerful song. The traveler was astonished and asked, "What are you doing?" The stonecutter looked up with a visionary gleam in his eye and said, "Can't you see? I am building a cathedral."

Same activity, totally different stories. Although often unconscious, all of us are constantly making up "parables" about our lives, stories we tell laden with all kinds of hidden morals or spiritual messages that give us a sense of purpose. Take away the story or change the story and suddenly the whole meaning behind our outer activities changes. Sometimes these shifts of meaning can be quite radical. Other times they are quite subtle. The point is whatever story you happen to be telling about a situation has a very large impact on your experience. Pause for a moment and ask yourself two questions:

"What are you doing with your life and your time?

And more importantly, what are the stories you tell yourself and others about what you are doing?"

Stories

In the midst of a three-day strategy session with the National Leadership Council of the US Forest Service (USFS), Harv and I were catching a quick bite to eat. As he recounted a story about his past I had heard several times before, the time felt right to interrupt his monologue. Putting my hand on his arm, I asked, "What would it take for you to put this old story down and simply offer what is yours right now, right here?" Abruptly redirecting the conversation jarred Harv out of the past and into the present. A smart and fast thinker, he struggled to make sense of what was happening. And then a flash of insight landed, he looked right at me and smiled.

Somewhere back along the way, he'd convinced himself he was an outsider and would never have credibility no matter how high he rose in the organization. Truth be told, he was well past being an outsider and held huge power and credibility he wasn't acknowledging or using. It was only his story that kept him from leading in the way he knew he could. That afternoon he raised his hand and volunteered to lead a deep and complex culture change process addressing old habits of employees engaging in unsafe behavior. Adding to an already very full plate of responsibilities, Harv led a small core team to design and deliver a half-day engagement process to all 40,000 employees. As a result of this process, new habits and mindsets were developed, and the USFS finally made real progress on a serious issue: annual fatalities. As a result of these efforts there was a dramatic and sustained drop in deaths.

Although Harv was one of many people, including four consecutive chiefs of the agency, who worked diligently over several years to arrive at zero fatalities, his leadership was instrumental in getting this huge effort off the ground and launched. And this new level of leadership began with a direct and concrete shift inside himself: he pivoted.

Pivoting

Pivoting, shifting your point of view on a given situation, is a skill all leaders know is crucial, yet often the act of doing it concretely remains elusive. The essence of pivoting is shifting the story being told—the story of self, the story of other, or the story of the situation. You can enter through any of these three "doorways." The key to each doorway is to name what you have heard as a story, rather than a fact set in stone, and get deeply curious about whether it is "true." With practice you will start noticing all the stories you tell. Noticing a story creates the possibility of stepping back from it and starting to look for alternative interpretations. Although conceptually this may sound easy, in practice there are two serious challenges to overcome.

The first challenge is presented by those stories we cling to fiercely and with certainty. Some stories are so close to home we cannot see alternatives no matter how hard we look. They are literally in our "blind spot." For these sorts of stories, it often takes someone else—a friend, colleague or bystander—to point out what we may not be seeing. Up comes the second challenge: what do we do when someone has the courage to offer us a hand out of our stuckness, to tell us something we may not want to hear? Overcoming both of these challenges is predicated on a basic assumption already being in place: *we are actually interested in questioning our stories and assumptions.* Often this is the root cause of being stuck in a point of view. It is a point of view we have spent years cultivating and do not want to give up without a fight. There is nothing particularly wrong with having a point of view worth fighting for; the problem comes when it is precisely this point of view keeping you stuck. Then you have to make a choice—keep it or change it.

In Harv's case, he didn't defend or deflect my comment. He took it in, rose to the occasion, and pivoted. For me, my first major lesson in "pivot and pivot fast" came during graduate school.

Blind Spots

I was twenty-nine and finishing up the final draft of my dissertation entitled "The Paradigm of the Universal Whole: Toward a New Theory of Personality." As part of my research, I used a well-known ego development test to verify if my working hypothesis was correct: individuals living in the spiritual community where I resided would score at the very high end of this test in terms of their ego development.

After I administered the test, the results came back, and the six subjects I tested were all over the place on the ego development scale. Because these results were the exact opposite of what I predicted, the conclusion I drew struck me as obvious. I had successfully proven that this longstanding and statistically validated ego development test was no longer valid and not an accurate measure for spiritually evolved people. As hard as it seems to believe, I was completely convinced my interpretation of the results was accurate!

Standing in front of my committee for the preliminary defense of my research, I got to the chapter regarding the ego development findings and proposed I had proven the test to be invalid. There was a distinct quiet in the room. Finally, one of my committee members cleared her throat and asked, "Did it ever occur to you that your working hypothesis might be wrong?"

Like a bolt of lightning running through my entire body, I suddenly realized the idea my hypothesis might be wrong had never crossed my mind. Turning a deep shade of red from head to toe, I had the most excruciating sensation of "burning up"—my young ego was being fried! After what felt like an eternity, I quietly said "No, actually, it hadn't crossed my mind that I might be wrong. I'll go back and rewrite this chapter."

Pivot and pivot fast. I went home and had no trouble rewriting the chapter. With my "blind spot" fully illuminated, it was easy to write up the exact opposite conclusion—my working hypothesis that "spiritually evolved" individuals would score at the high end of the test was wrong, not the test! I turned around a new draft in a week. A special footnote to this experience: a key concept advocated in my dissertation was the ability to shift your point of view instantly. In my final review, witnessing my practicing precisely what my dissertation was advocating without hesitation or defensiveness was a turning point for my committee. In the world of academia, this kind of rapid shift of hypothesis was a rare occurrence and one they all found very refreshing.

You Are Not Your Story

Three valuable lessons stand out from this experience: the importance of humility, staying present in the midst of discomfort, and the awareness that I am not *my story*. It's also a great teaching story highlighting the challenge of releasing opinions and storylines we've invested time, money, and effort creating. During a leadership training retreat for University of Colorado's Office of Research and Innovation, a new cohort of faculty fellows was sitting together discussing how difficult it is to change a point of view—your own or someone else's. Using my dissertation experience as illustrative of what it takes to truly pivot, the specific and personal nature of this skill came clear. In the moments of quiet following my story, one of the more introverted faculty members said abruptly "Oh, my god, I am not my hypothesis! I have never considered this before. . . . I really need to think about this!"

In the world of scholarly pursuits, where ideas and hypotheses are the very things you get known and paid for, shifting your hypothesis about a piece of research is not only challenging; it can be deeply destabilizing. Our identities are often totally wrapped up in our professional pursuits. Shifting our sense of identity beyond time spent in a work context can be difficult and raise deep fears as discussed in Chapter 8, unless you have cultivated a more internal point of reference. Remember the vertical axis of Being? This is your internal point of reference—a place that exists apart from the thoughts and feelings flowing through. Anchoring in this inner point of reference, it becomes possible to create a "gap"—a space of noticing our thoughts as simply thoughts. Like emotions, they come and then go like clouds floating through the sky. Not surprisingly, this kind of gap creation underlies many forms of meditation and mindfulness practices. It is in the gaps where breakthroughs occur in all walks of life, not only academia. An ancient skill long known to be critical to human beings' ability to adapt and survive.

Minding the Gap

Minding and mining this gap is the primary work of this direction: building a visceral and disciplined awareness of your Essential Self as distinct from the stories you tell and the opinions you form as a result. Stories are powerful because they hold both mental and emotional energy. When they move us toward learning, wholeness, and creativity, they can be invaluable. And yet often they create "prisons of our own making" where we sit and wonder why things aren't working or why our enthusiasm for living has dwindled. Unpacking, letting go of, updating, revising, and releasing old stories is the mojo of leadership. Telling your own stories and inviting others to share theirs is a place to begin.

Explore, Engage, Experiment

Storytelling is so effective because it activates the heart, which relaxes the mind. Creating contexts for sharing stories can be a goldmine of information and power. Small shifts in your own story or the stories in your organization, can create big shifts in action and behavior.

- *What are the stories you most frequently tell yourself?*
- *What are the stories you tell about your organization?*
- *What would need to shift in you to hear the possibility of a new story?*
- *If you had permission to tell a new story, where might you begin?*

As a simple structure for self and group reflection, story-telling can lead the way back to deeper questions of "Why?" and "To what end?" Connecting with the rich and life-changing elements of someone else's story, the precise key needed for our own next step drops into our hands.

Silence

As I waited for my husband to make a purchase at our local bookstore, a small book entitled *Listening below the Noise* caught my eye. I was looking for a light read when traveling, so I added it to the tab and slipped it into my briefcase when we got home. Settling into my airplane seat a few weeks later, I remembered this book, flipped it open, and began reading. Moments later tears were streaming down my cheeks—it was all I could do to contain a full-blown episode of weeping. *Not the place to read this book*, I thought. I closed it abruptly and returned it safely to my briefcase.

I put it on the coffee table at home. Several months passed before I decided to try it again. Sure enough, I barely got into the introduction when I started to cry. The opening pages describe a woman entering a "secret garden" where she has time and space to be with herself in a quiet way. Up from the watery depths bubbled the realization I was craving precisely this kind of time and space myself. Ignoring this message would have been unwise, the intense emotion was direct and unavoidable. I was being asked to "connect" (as described in Chapter 8)—connect to myself and my own inner voice.

Deliberate Immersion

At the heart of this book was the author's experience of *silence*—seventeen years of practicing every other Monday without fail. Each page was filled with her lived experience. Sensing the depth and beauty of Anne LeClair's experience, I decided to give it a try. One day a month dedicated to reconnecting with my own internal compass, creating space to hear and heed the nascent yet palpable impulses arising within myself. Gradually, the entire rhythm of my life transformed. Greater precision in my personal and professional choices. New levels of joy and relaxation. Everything rearranged around this one monthly practice.

My first day of silence was in March 2008. And I have kept his practice ever since—with an added twist. On retreat with five colleagues, we were considering the challenges and opportunities facing people and organizations with whom we worked. The theme of silence, solitude, and self-reflection surfaced. It was a need each of us felt individually and was being reflected by the increasing levels of anxiety, stress, fear and isolation we were seeing in our clients. Sharing my own experience, we decided to invite others to join in a monthly practice. A letter went out to our international networks, and the response was immediate. Over a thousand people now participate, men have joined what was originally a circle of women, and the network grows steadily each year. A monthly message of connection and inspiration goes out from Barbara Cecil and me to this network. A small seed growing quietly extends outward across the globe.[1]

Unplugging Regularly

Making time for silence and quiet self-reflection is an act of responsibility, not selfishness. It is also not a new subject of exploration. Back in the 1600s, the great philosopher and mathematician Blaise Pascal concluded, "All of humanity's problems stem from man's [and woman's] inability to sit quietly and alone." Inventions such as TV, smartphones, and the Internet did not suddenly create this avoidance; they simply continue to push us away from this practice rather than toward it. Stepping out of the fray takes discipline and commitment. Initially it may feel like you are swimming upstream against a mighty current. Take heart, small steps can yield big rewards.

You don't need to set aside hours or days and be sure you are in some remote setting to reap the rewards of this practice. During my years at Regis, I built in five to ten minutes of deliberate "unplugging" when I was in my office. Turning around in my chair, I would lean back, close my eyes, and shift my attention from work to myself, my breathing, and my body. If the phone rang, I would not answer it during this time. People passing in the hall could see into my office through a glass wall and from outside it most likely appeared I was sleeping. I didn't care. When the time was up, I would take a few final breaths and return to my work relaxed and refreshed.

Food for the Brain

As it turns out, these brief moments of silence are as good for the brain as they are for the soul. Neuroscientists have discovered that fifty-year-old meditators have the same amount of gray matter in their frontal cortex—the place in the brain linked to decision making and working memory—as people half their age. They also found shrinkage in the amygdala, a region of the brain associated with fear, anxiety, and aggression, which correlated with decreased levels of stress. And significant results could be seen with as little as fifteen to twenty minutes of meditation a day.[2] It is not about quantity as much as it is consistency and deliberate attention. As Louis L'Amour poetically writes:

"Long since I learned that one needs moments of quiet, moments of stillness, for both the inner and the outer man, a moment of contemplation or even simple emptiness when the stress could ease away and a calmness enter the tissues. Such moments of quiet gave one strength, gave one coolness of mind with which to approach the world and its problems. Sometimes but a few minutes were needed."[3]

Mental health and fluidity are deeply linked to building and sustaining a relationship with silence and solitude. Although it may not be easy at first, the rewards are real for both your own sense of sanity as well as your ability to lead with clarity and focus.

Explore, Engage, Experiment

Building a personal relationship and practice of silence—even if only for a few minutes a day or week or month—is a doorway to a new experience of your mind. Fear, anxiety, or agitation may well arise as you begin exploring this practice. Acknowledge these emotions, and they will gradually recede with time and practice. Start with small increments and build up your stamina over time— give yourself a few months or a year. *Pick a few minutes a day to experiment with silence. Start small and yet be consistent. Small steps taken regularly will grow into an experience of silence that lives below the noise.*

Try it and give it time to see what happens.

A Quiet Mind

As William Penn reminds us, *"True silence is the rest of the mind, and it is to the spirit what sleep is to the body, nourishment and refreshment."* In the same way a refreshed body is able to tackle the challenges of the day more effectively than a sleep-deprived body, a quiet mind is able to receive insight and new possibilities more readily than a mind spinning out of control.

Insight

When my husband and I got together, it was a scenario layered with complexity. I had lived in a spiritual community with 150 other people, including my husband's former wife, Susann, and their child. We had moved out of the community and into a small house in the town nearby where my seven-year-old stepdaughter would spend every other weekend with us. Not surprisingly, there was a great deal of tension in the relationships, and one of the manifestations was Susann choosing not to talk to me or interact with me in any direct way. After several months of this dynamic I noticed myself getting increasingly angry and agitated. Knowing this constant state of agitation was unhealthy, I reached for a solution. Finding one of my favorite pictures of Susann—she was and is a beautiful woman—I put it on a table by my bed and held the question, *"What do I need to understand or shift in myself to let this anger go?"*

The act of finding the picture, putting it by my bed, and asking the question was extremely difficult. It made me physically dizzy and nauseous, but I was determined to get this energy out of my body. Three days later, completely out of the blue, the message landed. Although the written words may sound trite, the phrase was:

She sees you as the enemy. And she may hate you for the rest of your life. Can you live with this?

As someone who prefers very much to have people like me rather than hate me, I felt this very direct insight like a crack in the middle of my forehead, and then came a deep sense of peace. *If she needs to hate me for the rest of my life then so be it. There is nothing I can do about that other than understand it and accept it.* These were the exact thoughts following upon the insight, and I accepted the truth and wisdom of them. My anger dissipated, replaced by a deep sense of calm.

Change in Self, Change in Other

The following day Susann called to make plans for the weekend and I happened to answer the phone. As though there were nothing problematic between us, she spoke to me cordially and directly. The tension had vanished! Almost dropping the phone, I thought perhaps this was my imagination or the change would be short lived. The months passed and things had, indeed, totally and completely shifted. Susann and I found our way to a spacious, respectful friendship that has remained over the ensuing decades.

The awareness of how genuinely "hard-wired" we are one to another has stayed with me since this experience. Knowing the profound impact my thinking has on both people and situations creates a new level of responsibility. Seeing the link between "change in self" leading to "change in other" squarely puts the onus in my own lap when things seem stuck, a realization as powerful as it is simple. And in the situation with Susann, it required letting go of many things: my need to be right and righteous, my judgments about her, my desire for her to change, and most of all, my desire to be liked. All these things shifted when the insight landed. Releasing these desires immediately opened space for something else to happen. The emergence of respect and spacious interaction—I believe—was a result of both her and my genuine openness.

Whether directly observed or not, *a shift of thought in one person will impact the other.* At times the shift may be mirrored back directly as happened with me and Susann. Other times no directly observable shifts seem apparent. Visible or not, your thoughts have impacted the whole. Whoever is the focus of your contemplations will experience you differently, even if you never say a word.

One-liners

An elegant simplicity is at work in direction of Mind. Insights come as "one-liners"—simple phrases blindingly obvious, which ring true. Before this happens, a situation seems complex and utterly unsolvable. Afterward, the solution is completely apparent and doable. Simplicity is a sign of the Mind rightly engaged, opening a path of clear and accurate direction. If things seem muddled and murky, it is simply not yet time to act. In the wise words of Ponca Chief White Eagle:

> *"When you're in doubt, be still, and wait;*
> *when doubt no longer exists for you,*
> *then go forward with courage.*
>
> *So long as mists envelop you, be still:*
> *be still until the sunlight pours through*
> *and dispels the mists—as it surely will.*
>
> *Then act with courage."*[4]

Action follows clear insight as surely as day follows night. Generating insight at an individual level has many parallels to breakthroughs occurring for a group of people.

Collective Insight

As the son of well-known preacher, Skip grew up in the heart of the civil rights movement. From an early age, he found himself in the midst of unfolding conversations—private and public. A rich history filled with stories, he told of a time when the movement had stalled and many of the leaders found themselves "enveloped in the mist."

It was the early 1960s. Although successes were occurring in bits and pieces, several key questions still persisted:

If you really wanted to communicate with large groups of people how would you do this?

How do you reach beyond the educated and the intelligentsia and extend a genuine invitation to all different segments of society?

What are we not seeing?

The normal paradigm of political organizing was still in operation: block-by-block, flyers with slogans, and connecting with organizations run and lead by men.

Fortunately, there were places people could gather, whites and blacks together, and sit with questions until a path forward appeared. One such place was The Highlander Folk School, a social justice leadership training school in Summerfield, Tennessee. Trained in these skills of mental fluidity, a group of community organizers were sitting with the above questions when into the midst of their collective quiet and openness came a clear and simple epiphany: "beauty parlors!"

Beauty parlors were the largest, naturally occurring network of connection within black communities all across the south. This network already existed. Owned and run by women, often with only two or three chairs per shop, the clientele was entirely black. Without threatening the momentum already moving for men—the churches, liberal colleges, and political leaders—for the first time the movement had a way to activate the voice of the women. Working-class women who were held in deep respect in every small community. When these women began to show interest and walked into the meetings in small clusters of two or three, everyone knew the momentum was moving again and this time it would be unstoppable. With this new groundswell of energy and participation, the March on Washington that had been envisaged would now become a reality.

Explore, Engage, Experiment

New insights come when you have *real questions,* questions for which you and others genuinely have no immediate answer. Sitting with these questions and not rushing to a quick answer can take time but when insight comes it usually a total game changer.

- *What are your real questions?*
- *If you cannot think of any questions, ask yourself, what aspects of this world stir your curiosity?*
- *If you didn't have to figure out an answer quickly, what questions might you want to entertain, to hold and to ponder?*

Letting the answer come requires a mind open and willing to listen. A lovely and powerful book *A More Beautiful Question: The Power of Inquiry to Spark Breakthrough Ideas*[5] can be a useful resource as you search for real questions to every aspect of your life.

Relaxed and Open

The heart of mental fluidity is relaxation, not struggling or trying to force an answer. Knowing the universe will deliver, often when you least expect it. As the saying goes, "I get my best insights when I am in the shower or out for a run!" In these moments the "struggling" has been put on the back burner and the mind automatically relaxes like a calm and tranquil lake into which a single pebble is thrown. *Kerplunk!* In drops insight from which a new action can ripple toward the shore.

Getting Traction

A relaxed and open mind creates the conditions for releasing old stories, pivoting quickly and receiving new insights. Embracing the gap, the awareness "you are not your thoughts," is central. When the vertical axis of Being is in place, the "you" doing the thinking finally has choice. You can choose which thoughts to entertain and which are best left alone. And as has been said many times, thoughts carry great power and where you focus them matters!

An old Cherokee chief was teaching
his grandson about life. . . .

"A fight is going on inside me," he said to the boy.
"It is a terrible fight and it is between two wolves.

"One is evil—he is anger, envy, sorrow, regret,
greed, arrogance, self-pity, guilt, resentment, inferiority,
lies, false pride, superiority, self-doubt, and ego.

*"The other is good—he is joy, peace, love, hope,
serenity, humility, kindness, benevolence, empathy,
generosity, truth, compassion, and faith.*

*"This same fight is going on inside you—
and inside every other person, too."*

*The grandson thought about it for a
minute and then asked his grandfather,
"Which wolf will win?"*

*The old chief simply replied,
"The one you feed."*

Which thoughts will win? Whichever ones you feed. Seen
in this way, you have room to engage with thoughts fluidly
and creatively. With patience, time, and discipline, the payoffs
for this work are substantial: lightness, humor, and curiosity become the dominant experiences in place of frustration,
irritation, and anxiety.

Rewriting the stories of your life and reframing intractable situations are two muscle-building practices in this direction. Progress is occurring when a new level of humor and lightness comes into your living. Although it is serious business on one level, you learn to give yourself a break at another. Freedom to be you increases, and the need to be perfect without foibles, blind spots, and stuck places decreases. Ponder the experience of lightness and humor in your life. Use the following questions as starting points for self-reflection:

- *Are there places where you feel heaviness?*
- *If so, how might you rewrite the story you are carrying to lighten the load?*
- *Can you course correct and pivot quickly and with a sense of ease?*
- *Where do you find yourself getting defensive?*
- *How could you reframe the situation to see it differently?*

Chapter 11:

North: Embrace Your

Spiritual Destiny

○◇◇◇◇◇◇◇◇◇◇◇◇◇◇◇◇◇◇◇◇◇◇◇◇◇◇◇◇◇◇◇○

*"Everything on earth has a purpose, every disease an
herb to cure it, and every person a mission. This is
the Indian theory of existence."*
                              —CHRISTAL QUINTASKET, SALISH

*K*laus, an internationally renowned master of horsemanship, wrote his first book while living in an abandoned
outhouse. At the time, he was in massive debt and a complete
unknown to the world of horses. In his early thirties, he was
searching for next steps and found himself living with and
learning about horses. Immersing himself, in two short years
he developed a deep understanding of these incredible animals. Because he realized his ways of communicating with
horses were new and unique, he wrote a book encapsulating
his experiences. Catching a wave soon to become global, the
book took hold and revolutionized people's understanding of
horses. In his own words, he recounted these early moments:

"I wrote my first book while sitting on a piece of ply-wood I had nailed across the holes of the outhouse. This was both my office and my bed at the time. I knew I needed to write this book, and it came very quickly. I wrote the entire book in two months.

"I sought out three different potential publishers. The first two wouldn't even meet with me because I was a complete unknown. The third agreed. After we sat down together, he became intrigued. I asked for an advance—a very sizable one at the time—and he wanted some kind of guarantee for the risk he was assuming, particularly as he heard the whole story of my situation.

"I said to him, 'Look into my eyes. I guarantee you this book will be an instant bestseller and will change the world of horsemanship.'"

Klaus's audacity and confidence captivated the publisher, who shook hands and wrote a large check. And the world pivoted for both of these men. The book became an instant international bestseller and still is almost thirty years later. This success gave Klaus a platform for his work in the world of horsemanship and also changed the course of the publisher's life and work. They remained close friends up until the publisher's death.

Destiny

Although Klaus's story can seem extreme, it is often how destiny comes calling. Old ways of living no longer work, and you land in challenging, new, or unpredictable territory. Klaus was in massive debt and living in an outhouse! Yet it is moments like these when taking a leap of faith and risking it all in pursuit of a deep compulsion cracks open new possibilities. Initially, your actions may appear borderline crazy. Leaving a potentially secure position because in your gut it feels right. You know a change is needed. Or a line of work dries up, and you are forced to head in a new direction. There are myriad ways destiny calls. The one thing for certain is destiny calls. The question is, are you willing to meet it when it does?

Doors Close, Doors Open

I made a bet with my high school field hockey coach I'd be a doctor by the time I turned thirty. A fifty-dollar bet, which I ended up winning but not as I had imagined. Pre-med classes were the focus of my early college years. For my first work-study semester, l landed a six-month stint in a large rehabilitation unit in a Seattle hospital. As the months went by, I began to feel suffocated and depressed. Working in a hospital day in and day out raised serious doubts about my career choice. However, I'd invested a lot of time, money, energy, and intention in this direction, so I persevered. Upon graduation I took the MCAT, the required medical school entrance exam, and I totally bombed the exam. Enrolling in an intensive, three-month crash course in passing the MCAT, I studied my brains out and took the exam again. And this time I did worse!

Completely confused with no idea what to do next, I took a job teaching rock climbing and kayaking in Colorado for the summer. It was a good way to earn some money, be outdoors, and forget about medical school for the time being.

Summer turned into fall, and a new job with a different outdoor leadership school opened up. Fall turned into a three-month winter job. Unbeknownst to me, a deep piece of my destiny was beginning to unfold. Two decades later I had run wilderness-based leadership programs around the world, raised money to start leadership schools in South Africa as well as Bulgaria, and gotten my PhD in human and organizational development. I did become a doctor, just not a medical doctor! Gradually my life turned toward a totally different career landscape much more suited to my own inherent loves and aptitudes. I needed one door to close, failing my MCAT, so destiny could get me pointed in the right direction.

Doors close so others can open. Moving in apparently "random" directions, our lives will guide us to those things we're meant to do. Sometimes this guidance takes the form of "trial and error." Testing options, harvesting the gifts, and slowly honing in on ever more accurate ways to contribute. Make no mistake, you do have gifts to claim and live into. The key question is, *Will you claim them?* Claiming my love of the natural world and all things wild seemed too "fun and frivolous" to be an actual gift. And yet this love informs and inspires virtually every aspect of the way I teach, coach and, consult. *What is it you love?*

Find the Thread

We all have a "thread"—our piece to weave in the world without which the ecosystem of life would be diminished. Living in concert with destiny is all about perceiving the thread, letting it guide your choices during good times and difficulties.

> *There's a thread you follow. It goes among*
> *things that change. But it doesn't change.*
> *People wonder about what you are pursuing.*
> *You have to explain about the thread.*
> *But it is hard for others to see.*
> *While you hold it you can't get lost.*
> *Tragedies happen; people get hurt*
> *or die; and you suffer and get old.*
> *Nothing you do can stop time's unfolding.*
> *You don't ever let go of the thread.*
> —WILLIAM STAFFORD[1]

People who have kept ahold of their "thread" have a certain kind of magic, a palpable brightness about them. For me, few people epitomize this magic more than my friend Jody.

Shortly after moving to New Hampshire, we were invited to a neighbor's house for tea. Sitting in her living room was another couple who had also just moved to town—the Simpsons. As she extended her hand in greeting, it was clear Jody and I were destined to meet. Little did I know what a model she would become for a life well-lived.

Jody grew up surrounded by music. Although her dad was a banker and her mother a wife and homemaker, they both loved music. He would play the clarinet and she the piano, filling the home with beautiful music and relaxation. Like a sponge, Jody soaked it up, and soon began seeking out every opportunity she could find to sing. All through school and into college, she warbled away. Without thinking about it or noticing consciously, she had her thread firmly in hand.

As part of the early class of women at Dartmouth, she created a female singing group called the Dartmouth Distractions, an a cappella octet who performed all over the region and ended up on TV. For these efforts she received the MacDonald-Smith music prize. When she married and had children, the role of music needed to get even more sharply focused. As she said, "Whatever I chose to do had to be so worth it to justify leaving my children. It had to be intense and something I totally loved to do; otherwise I was not going to get a babysitter and take time away from my family."

Creating ways to sing with her children, she began to include other children. Through a series of synchronistic events and hard work, Jody ended up at the New England Conservatory of Music, where she became a conductor and launched one of the most renowned and successful children's choirs in the country, Performing Artists at Lincoln School (PALS). At the request of conductor Seiji Ozawa, this choir performed on many occasions with the Boston Symphony at major venues including Tanglewood and Carnegie Hall. Maestro Ozawa and Jody shared a love for the irrepressible spirit of children.

When it came time to let PALS go and move to this little town of Hancock, she simply brought her magic with her. Over the last fourteen years, she's created Norway Pond Festival Singers, Junior Minstrels, and Music on Norway Pond. She has singers who range in age from four to eighty! Superstars and world-renowned musical groups come here at her invitation. Concerts are packed with people from across the Monadnock region—people of all political and religious persuasions from across the economic spectrum. Building community through music, she is a master of her craft. And she draws those with other gifts to walk side-by-side with her creating a ripple effect across New England.

A Tapestry of Contribution

Our threads need the threads of others to be strong and resilient. In Jody's story, she drew specific individuals whose gifts were different from hers and absolutely essential for her magic to unfold. Nancy took care of all PALS's administrative needs and Bret was their brilliant pianist/accompanist, allowing Jody to focus on the children and the music. This is always the case. We are never alone in our work of tapestry weaving.

Your destiny works in concert and in complement with others. This is the artistry and beauty of living in this way—you never need to be the whole enchilada. If it is not people, it will be some other part of creation: animals, plants, rocks, rivers. The raw materials for creating magic are all around. Opening yourself to the widest range of potential resources can assist in not only keeping ahold of your own thread but seeing clearly how it weaves with others.

There is nothing random about your gifts and the ways they are meant to contribute to the whole. As John O'Donohue describes:

> *"To be born is to be chosen. For millions of years, before you arrived here, the dream of your individuality was carefully prepared. You were sent to a shape of destiny in which you would be able to express the special gift you bring to the world."*[2]

Lean into the idea of being "dreamed" before being born. Notice the people, places, and activities that light you up. Don't fret. You cannot "not be you." Destiny is always at work, tracking us down even when we might try to hide. As Carl Jung reminds us: "One finds destiny on the path one takes to avoid it!" There really is no getting away, there are only degrees of struggle. You can end up creating a bit of a "shroud" around yourself unconsciously, or sometimes consciously putting on masks and veils. But know with certainty, you are always present, living the life you were destined to live as best as you can in every moment. A simple curiosity is almost all that is required to activate a greater precision about how, when, where, and with whom to share your unique way of being in the world. Hold questions and wait for insights. There is no rush and no right answer.

Explore, Engage, Experiment

There is a thread to follow, to hold and nurture, keeping you close with Destiny. For some, the thread is relatively obvious and the following two questions may work well:

- *What is this thread for you?*
- *How does it serve as a guiding force in your life?*

If you find difficulty with the questions above, try the following:

- *Ask three friends you know and trust what they see as your unique qualities of character.*
- *What do they see you do naturally and assume everyone else does this too?*
- *Think of three different situations or events where you were truly at your best. Write or tell someone a brief story about each one. Review the stories. See if you can find a pattern or essence of similarity among them.*

Embedded in the threads of destiny are clues to the natural and powerful way you lead. For most of us, leadership is a word meant for others, for those in outer positions of authority. We don't see the leadership already flowing through us into the world. What about embracing the idea that every single person has a leadership gift to offer?

Gifts

Ross is a senior vice president in a very successful financial services company. Dialogos was called in when this company hit a major crisis and several of the founders were transitioned out. Ross was one of a dozen managers needing to step up into this leadership void. Looking around the room, I spied him sitting quietly in the background and immediately thought, *There is a real leader over there, but he doesn't know it yet!* His particular strengths were almost the opposite of many of those in current leadership roles. Rather than being gregarious, outgoing, and effusive, he was quiet, reserved, and introspective. Keen powers of observation and the ability to ask real and critical questions were two of his gifts. These gifts along with others were instinctual, intuitive, and automatic, making them virtually invisible to Ross. My job was helping him "see himself accurately." To see the way he naturally led and interrupt the story line he carried: "Well that is nothing special, doesn't everyone do X?" And the answer is a definitive "No, not everyone does X, you do!"

Gradually embracing these gifts, he stopped trying to make himself be something he was not meant to be. He began using keen and astute questions as his point of entry. Rather than withholding his observations until someone asked him what he thought, he started sharing them of his own accord. Not so everyone would necessarily agree, but so his angle on the situation and the decisions could be used as valuable information. Freed up from old models of leadership, he offered his wisdom and insight directly, moving out of the wings and into the midst of the ongoing decision-making processes. As a result, when a vacancy opened up on the leadership team of the company, Ross was tapped to take it.

In addition to the personal shifts, Ross also noticed an

organizational "mindset shift" occurring. "At the start, we all saw coaching as 'repair work'—if you had a coach, it meant you were having problems. What none of us considered at the beginning was we were being coached to open up even greater potential. The company evolved from a 'repair mindset' to an 'investment mindset.' Seeing people as future leaders, we began to figure out what their gifts were and invest in their development. As a result, the culture now encourages different voices and empowers others more readily." With this mindset shift, it became much easier to see the untapped potential in others and make space for them to share their gifts too.

Seeing the Gifts in Others

Relaxing and valuing your idiosyncratic leadership strengths creates the conditions for others to show up and be valued. Use your own confidence to unlock stuck situations and invite waiting players into the game. Seek out a different view, an unusual voice. Ask the person in the corner who has not said a word what they think about a situation. Anchor your professional work to an honest assessment of your own capabilities, and this will draw natural talent from those around you. It will also generate ever greater precision around the best and highest use of your talents.

When your own gifts are alive and flourishing, it becomes easier to inspire those with whom you work. The link between inspiration and output is clear. Engaging and including people will give you better than average output. However, creating a workforce of truly inspired people generates a level of productivity over twice the average.[3] Tapping this deeper potential is high-leverage work that is most often undertaken by individuals who are truly inspired themselves. This level of inspiration is born by holding a "creative tension," where the steady urgings toward new and unchartered territory stay balanced with deep perception and patience.

Holding Creative Tension

James was a bright, young director at a large and prestigious international finance and development organization. Over time he cultivated a highly successful leadership team and delivered impressive returns in his division. The only options upward were a few select vice presidential slots. Sought after when these jobs came up, most people jumped and remained in place for years afterward. Twice James was offered a vice presidency, and twice he declined. He was waiting and listening for a job squarely aligned with the work he was meant do in the world. Although he would have most likely been successful in whatever job he chose, he had learned to listen for opportunities that truly excited him. Clear and confident about his gifts, he passed on jobs when others said, "Are you crazy?" When an opportunity arrived totally aligned with his destiny, he said "Yes!" and moved on to a new organization. Total precision. The new job had much more scope and scale than any of the vice-presidential opportunities in the organization he left. Using both courage and discernment, James found his next opportunity to contribute his gifts in service of the whole.

Leadership gifts are not random, they are precise. Serving as guides and allies, they help us make clear personal and professional choices, staying put until the moment is right and then moving with conviction and assurance. Knowing when to say "Yes" and when to say "No, thank you."

Explore, Engage, Experiment

Life presents us with choices daily. Explore the choices you are making. Think about recent choices as well as future options, if there are any on the horizon. Use these few questions as starting points for moving toward choices which bring you alive.

- *Are you waking up inspired by the work you are doing?*
- *Do you feel you are using the gifts that are most natural to you?*
- *If not, what is one next step that you could take to move yourself more closely toward using your inherent talents?*

Talents are linked to inspiration, and inspiration is linked to the feeling of joy. Joy is a sure sign you and destiny are dancing together and is the fourth primary emotion in the suite of emotional agility.

Joy

"The place God calls you to is the place where your deep gladness and the world's deep hunger meet."
—FREDERICK BUECHNER

After years of creating wilderness-based leadership schools in various parts of the world, it was time for a job closer to home. Thorne Ecological Institute, a well-known but struggling environmental education organization, was a perfect fit for transitioning to something new. I accepted the job as executive director with one condition: a shortened work week. Three-quarter time with full benefits. They were taken aback—this was well before the benefits of the four-day work week started making their way into the mainstream press—but I was clear this was nonnegotiable.

A three-day weekend made all the difference. Focused, energized, and enjoying this new opportunity, I made some critical staff changes, and the financial challenges straightened out quickly. Turning things around was relatively simple; the greater issue was ensuring long-term stability. As destiny would have it, a nearby wetland Thorne wanted to conserve became the key to success. With the help of Colleen, another intrepid believer that "nothing is impossible," we created a multi-stakeholder partnership between Thorne, the City of Boulder, and the Boulder County School District. Through this partnership, Sombrero Marsh, a forty-five-acre wetland, was preserved and turned into a permanent home for Thorne. With this as its base of operations, Thorne expanded its science education to hundreds of children annually throughout Boulder County. A relatively simple project, leveraging key strengths from three different organizations, built a legacy sustainable for the long term.

Legacies

Legacies most often have "reciprocity" built into the fabric of their creation: partnerships that succeed because the unique gifts of each member are allowed to flourish. Reciprocity is a natural by-product of work in sync with destiny. Use it as a guiding premise. Listen for where to invest your precious time and energy. As the stoic Seneca said, "Life is long if you know how to use it." How you use your time is the difference between *existing* versus *living*. Let joy be your guide and daily acts be the focus.

Long-term legacies are built one step at a time, and your own health and well-being are included as a part of the process. The notion of sacrificing yourself for the good of the whole is not a part of this way of leading. Although at times it may appear to others your way of living is a sacrifice, when the choices are in sync with destiny, this is not the actual experience.

Small Seed, Big Impact

Born in pre-partitioned India, Abdul Sattar Edhi migrated to Pakistan and worked as a cloth seller. He lived off commission from selling clothes and begging. And he begged for a purpose—to feed the poor.

Abdul founded his welfare trust—which is Pakistan's biggest—with only fifty dollars. He was a true giver. Rescuing over 20,000 infants who were abandoned, his work provided the basic necessities—food, shelter, and education—to over 50,000 orphans, and free training to more than 40,000 nurses. He started 330 welfare trusts in the country and was renowned for operating the largest ambulance service in the world—comprising of 24/7 service with 1,500 vehicles!

These welfare trusts ran numerous rehabilitation centers, shelter homes, and food kitchens for children, women, the disabled, and the underprivileged. He traveled to the US, Europe, and Africa on many relief missions, including sites affected by Hurricane Katrina. For all his selfless deeds, Abdul was never recognized with a Nobel Peace Prize, nor did he seek one.

Consistent with his way of living and message, Abdul never had a house or car of his own. All he survived with was a charpai (a small woven bed frame), a chair, and a desk, which was a gift from his friend. He had no money after his death, donated his organs, and parted from the world with the following words: "Take care of the poor people of my country!"[4]

Known to Those You Serve

Engaging and surrounding himself with hundreds of thousands of people in poverty was Adbul Edhi's destiny and his gladness. A story with a clear and obvious legacy of meeting needs in the world, yet I suspect very few people in the United States have ever heard of him. This is most often the way of destiny. We're known to those we are meant to serve. To the rest of the world, we are invisible. Sometimes our impact is felt long after we are dead and gone. The famous painter Vincent Van Gogh died penniless and unrecognized. It was not until much later that his work was appreciated and valued. You may never know most of the people impacted by your life. This is a good thing. Enjoy this and let your life unfold in accordance with a will and intelligence far beyond your own. We can all get paralyzed by wanting to make a difference but all we see in front of us are options seemingly small and insignificant.

Destiny starts small:

- ○ *Abdul founded his trust with fifty dollars*
- ○ *I bombed my MCATS*
- ○ *Klaus wrote a book while living in an abandoned outhouse*
- ○ *Jody sang around the piano with her parents*

It is embedded in your DNA: your spiritual signature, your birthright. If someone else could do your gift, they would be here instead of you. My friend Sy is a well-known author who writes about animals and develops profound connections with them—the latest being an octopus! I could never live the life Sy has crafted, and she could not live mine. Each of us is pulled to do something unique in the world, and one gift is not better or more significant than another. The art is steadily discerning what to put your attention toward and what to leave for others. This kind of discernment is not an intellectual exercise; it is an experience of the heart:

> *"Certain things will catch your eye, but pursue only those that capture your heart."*
> —ANCIENT NATIVE AMERICAN PROVERB

A Path of the Heart

Destiny is a path of the heart, and when it is chosen and walked, we connect deeply with the emotion of joy. However, it is a joy born of active and ongoing discipline and choice-making. It requires us to live with all seven directions engaged and often asks us to do things in direct and stark contradiction to the norms of our culture, our upbringing, and all the messages bombarding us daily. In many respects, it means living on the edge of what you know to be true and always being willing to question what was a given the day before.

> *"Make no mistake, this kind of unconditional joy does not come easily. It requires transcending our human limitations and facing our cultural shadows. It demands discipline, accountability, and a profound attunement with Divine Will."*
> —ANDREW HARVEY[5]

Your gifts come from the universe itself. Using them in service to the well-being of the whole awakens an unconditional experience of joy—joy which is possible because it is dancing with all the other emotions too. It is a kind of joy which honors a fundamental grace which lives in all of creation. When embraced this kind of joy can call out the gifts in those with whom you come in contact. Because you are anchored deeply to the whole, this experience flows out to others, inviting them to join you in their own unique way.

Explore, Engage, Experiment

Joy joins Sadness, Anger, and Fear as a primary emotion of the heart. In the same way the other emotions find real and genuine expression without being overinflated or repressed, so it is with joy. Destiny is dynamic. It will ask you to embrace the full range of emotions on the journey. And it offers the genuine opportunity to experience a calm and relaxed quality of joy. Here are three questions to contemplate:

- *What truly brings you joy?*
- *What would be at risk for you to pursue this?*
- *What would be at risk if you don't?*

Getting Traction

Over time, my ability to discern the actions and directional clues in line with my destiny have gotten ever more precise. Many lessons came as the result of contrast, noticing the qualitative difference in my experience when my essential gifts were being used and when they weren't. It would be easy to dwell in the land of regret for the times I seemed some distant version of myself, either trying to please someone else or trying to live up to some self-created image. However, the way seems far gentler to me now. *In truth we are always on our path, no matter how circuitous the journey may seem.* As I said recently to my stepdaughter, who is going through her own moment of apparent life crisis, we are always in the river of life even when it feels like we are not. Truth is you cannot sit on the bank, but you can sit in an eddy, a protected spot in the river, usually behind a big rock where the water moves quietly back upstream and holds you in place. But you are still in the river; you are simply taking some time to ponder your next moves before you get back into the major current and see where the river will take you.

Having been a kayaker and taught kayaking, I find coming out of an eddy can sometimes be really difficult, and when you finally catch the current again, things can happen fast. It can feel both exhilarating and terrifying simultaneously! Fear not. Have faith. Stay closely connected to your thread—the small fractal of the web of life that is yours. Learn how to navigate the river rather than fighting against it. At some point it begins to feel like play, and the ride becomes much more enjoyable.

A quality of quiet contentment lives inside when your outer work lines up with your inner gifts. An experience of *ordinariness* comes. Life feels natural and unpretentious. It is no big deal. If you find you've stopped pushing or pulling or struggling to somehow fit in, perhaps you are sitting squarely in the path of destiny. A lack of struggle, a sense of ease, and a relaxation with the small piece of creation that is yours to tend can all be used as metrics to confirm you are making progress in this direction.

PART FOUR:

Rebuilding Community

Chapter 12:

Return to We

o—×××××××××××××××××××××××××××××××—o

*"You see, there is no "I" alone in the speaking of our
people. When referring to another among us, as when
referring to ourselves, we speak in "we."*
—Anasazi Foundation, The Seven Paths: Changing
One's Way of Walking in the World

*I*n celebration of my parents' sixtieth wedding anniversary,
ten members of my family walked to a sunny spot behind
the house—the house of my grandmother which is now my
home. Cradled in my arms was a small cedar of Lebanon
tree I had ordered especially for this occasion. Cedar of Lebanon trees are known for longevity, and although they're not
native to New Hampshire, the climate is conducive for them
to thrive. Standing in a circle of three generations, each one
took turns with the shovel making a hole the right size for
this small tree. Scattering cornmeal in the hole, along with
plenty of fish emulsion and fertilizer, we planted the tree and
attached small supports to keep it growing straight while
the roots found purchase in the ledge and rocks below. My

brother suggested we sing a song of blessing. Out came a simple tune we could all learn easily and sing together.

Getting ready to go back inside, I picked up my shovel and turned toward the house. Pausing, my father looked back at the tree and said with a wry smile, "No pressure on that little tree!"

Like this little tree planted as a celebration and a reminder of the gradual unfolding of life over multiple generations, this final chapter is a reminder that the "I," the unfolding self for which you are responsible, is squarely embedded in the "we." As was mentioned earlier, human beings are tribal by nature, and when we try to live as solitary beings, big parts of us wither and die. In honor of this truth, here are three parting images to hold as you walk this path.

Seven Generations

"The true meaning of life is to plant trees under whose shade you never expect to sit."

—NELSON HENDERSON

Planting a tree, virtually any kind of tree, inherently honors past, current, and future generations. As I care for this fifty-five acres of woodlands passed down from my grandmother to my father and then on to me, it is impossible to think only in terms of one lifetime. Red oaks, one of the main trees in our woods, don't reach their prime for at least 150 or 200 years. Lightly stewarding the land to support these statuesque trees requires careful thought and planning. They provide critical food and habitat for the local wildlife, not to mention wood for heating our home each winter. As teachers, they are helping cultivate a multigenerational stance inside myself. This stance needs to be reawakened in us all and included as part of our ongoing decision-making processes.

In today's world, where information arrives in nano-seconds and success or failure is often measured in months rather than years or decades, taking the longer view will require building new habits and also learning from those who are already well-versed in this way of living. When Tibet was still its own country, there was a rule that anyone proposing a new invention had to guarantee it was beneficial, or at least harmless, to seven generations of humans before it could be adopted. In native and indigenous cultures both historically and today, their traditions have always included considering the consequences for at least seven generations:

*What will the impact of this decision
be on my children's children?*

*Do my actions and choices create a more healthy,
sustainable, and life-giving planet?*

*Are my choices regarding "x" (this land, this
home, these resources) strengthening basic ecosystem
needs such as water, air, habitat, diversity?*

Patience, observation, and thoughtfulness characterize this stance of seven generations. Implications for leading and leadership in the context of a multigenerational view become intriguing to ponder. Think about the classic business phrase, "Whatever you measure is what you make progress on." *What would we begin to measure if we embraced seven generations as the metric?*

Although I don't know the answer to this question, it is an important question to begin asking. In traditional cultures, it was and is still often the role of the elders to hold questions like this. Elders are those who knew and still know how to hold the whole, hold divergent views, and listen deeply and patiently for wisdom and guidance. We need more elders, people of all ages and stages from all races and traditions who can hold the long arc of time and listen for the real and serious answers to all the questions being raised by a way of living that appears to be collapsing across the globe.

Growing Elders

The presence and respect for elders is alive and well in various indigenous cultures around the world. Maintaining and restoring balance is one of their key roles. For example, when someone does something wrong, they see it as a collective and community issue not solely an individual issue. Healing then becomes the process of letting go—physically, mentally, emotionally, and spiritually— of *our* hurt—the hurt that has been inflicted upon each of us, the hurt that we have inflicted upon others . . . Healing occurs by replacing our anger, our guilt, our shame, our vulnerability, with the seven teachings: honesty, love, courage, truth, wisdom, humility and respect. They unite as a community to restore the balance.[1]

Imagine how different your life might have been if the first time you did something for which you were ashamed or embarrassed there was a way to bring it to the community for healing. Trying, testing, and making mistakes are not only the hallmarks of growing up, they are also the hallmarks of continuing to explore the boundaries of your life. And when you hit the wall, when you fall on your face, you definitely need others to remind you all is okay, you are still loved and valued. Although this can be done by close friends, parents, and siblings if they are mature enough to hold you in this way, real tension and challenge arises when our mistakes impact others in our community or the world at large. Holding a person or persons when serious mistakes get made used to be the domain of village elders, people who could hold seemingly opposite points of view with equanimity, understanding, and wisdom while the root issues of the conflict could be surfaced and resolved.

Growing your capacity to be an elder, to hold all the challenges and complexities of this world is the essence of Leadership Flow. Become an adult. Own your experience and enlarge your sense of things.

In a Hindu parable, an aging master grew tired of his apprentice complaining, and so, one morning, sent him for some salt. When the apprentice returned, the master instructed the unhappy young man to put a handful of salt in a glass of water and then to drink it. "How does it taste?" the master asked.

"Bitter," spat the apprentice.

The master chuckled and then asked the young man to take the same handful of salt and put it in the lake. The two walked in silence to the nearby lake, and once the apprentice swirled his handful of salt in the water, the old man said, "Now drink from the lake."

As the water dripped down the young man's chin, the master asked, "How does it taste?" "Fresh," remarked the apprentice. "Do you taste the salt?" asked the master. "No," said the young man.

At this, the master sat beside this serious young man who so reminded him of himself and took his hands, saying, "The pain of life is pure salt; no more, no less. The amount of pain in life remains the same, exactly the same. But the amount of bitterness we taste depends on the container we put the pain in.

So when you are in pain, the only thing you can do is to enlarge your sense of things . . . stop being a glass. Become a lake.[2]

Become a lake. Embrace the skills that allow you to hold space and find solutions to the deep divides and polarizations arising as a normal and natural result of human nature. Honor those already doing the work of eldering, already rebuilding communities at both a micro as well as macro scale. And when you meet these individuals, bow to their wisdom and let yourself be deeply inspired.

Rebuilding Communities

I met Francisco de Roux in 2008 when he was invited to be a guest presenter to Dialogos's Leadership for Collective Intelligence (LCI) program. Francisco is known as the "guerilla priest." Much of his life's work has been with the victims of Colombia's decades-long armed conflict between the state, which claims to be fighting for stability and order and FARC, a guerilla movement claiming to be fighting for the rights of the poor. Between 1964 and 2019 more than three million people have been displaced and about 220,000 people have died, four out of five of them noncombative civilians. As part of a 2016 peace deal, a Commission for the Clarification of Truth, Coexistence, and Non-Repetition was set-up and in May 2018 began its work headed by de Roux.

Francisco spent decades engaging with the pain and suffering occurring throughout Colombia; in all corners, all social groups, and all levels of society. As a Jesuit priest, his life has been dedicated to seeing the "essential person" and separating this from the heinous deeds they may have committed. Through his work, victims and perpetrators have been able to talk together about reconciliation and structural changes in the country, working together to make Colombian society better for all.[3]

Sitting with our small group of leaders on the coast of Maine, he shared his experiences and wisdom. His presence exudes a calm and vibrant aliveness. As the two hours unfolded, an atmosphere of deep and authentic engagement was created. When the session closed, the whole group sat in silence. So much had been stirred at such profound levels, we canceled all formal sessions for the remainder of the day, giving time for people to be alone or in small groups sharing, thinking, and simply sitting together.

Francisco epitomizes the seven directions in action. In his presence, inner stillness meets outer precision. He is vitally alive and deeply relaxed. He can hold all manner of atrocities and interact with people from all walks of life. Because of his personal mastery, he is able to help rebuild community across deep, painful divisions. This is the leadership work of our times. It happens one person at a time, one community at a time, through the efforts of each of us embodying our own version of this way of living.

We Are All Needed

Regard heaven as your father, Earth as your mother, and all things as your brothers and sisters."
—NATIVE AMERICAN PROVERB

Examples such as de Roux remind us of the deep, essential nature of each person. Although our differences can divide us, in truth they were meant to unite and strengthen the fabric of the whole not tear it apart. Own your place in the whole. Learn how to dance with others in service to our collective humanity. Remember all those who came before you and are supporting you whether you know it or not. In the words of renown arctic photographer and explorer Camille Seaman:

"You are billions of years in the making, and you carry the wisdom of your ancestors inside you. You

can access this at any time. You are born of this time, for this time, and there is no one like you. And you must do what you were put here to do uniquely. And your job is to figure out what that is."[4]

At times each of us loses sight of this profound truth—we feel lost, wandering without a sense of connection or purpose. It is these times we all need community—someone, somewhere to remind us we are not alone. We are never alone no matter how deeply we believe this to be true. Embedded in the vast web of creation, bathed in the wonder and resilience of this planet, we are in community with all that is. When we remember this truth is when we truly return to *we*:

> *"We are each here for a reason,*
> *and we are all needed."*

Appendix:

Indigenous Ways of Knowing:
A beginning list of resources

⊙∞∞∞∞∞∞∞∞∞∞∞∞∞∞∞⊙

Mankiller, Wilma. *Every Day is a Good Day*. Golden, CO: Fulcrum Publishing.

An honest and rare book into the resilience, wisdom, and perseverance of Native American women. Sharing stories about spirituality, traditions and culture, patterns of thought, and shared values, it resounds with humor and strategies for survival in a context where the degradation of indigenous societies has been systematic and virtually unacknowledged.

Wagamese, Richard. *Keeper 'n Me*. Toronto, Canada: Penguin Random House.

By turns funny, poignant, and mystical, this novel based on historical events casts a fresh and powerful light on the redemptive power of community, tradition, and the process of coming home to self in the deepest sense of these words.

Kimmerer, Robin Wall. *Braiding Sweetgrass: Indigenous Wisdom, Scientific Knowledge, and the Teachings of Plants.* Minneapolis, MN: Milkweed Editions.

A beautiful and wise book filled with an awareness of the connection between living things and of the vibrant world we inhabit. It is written as a celebration of our reciprocal relationship with all creation.

Stan Rushworth Interview. https://bit.ly/3cM1ZBm

An interview with Native American historian, teacher, and elder Stan Rushworth discussing the schism between Western worldviews and the deep realities of indigenous life. Acknowledging the past, present, and future possibilities of finding our ways toward real and authentic engagement, Stan underscores the need for long-term education and an honest reckoning with our country's history if we are to come to any kind of a new future together.

Additional Resources in Each Direction

Above: Trust Life

La Chapelle, David. *Hymn of Changes: Contemplations of the I Ching.* Princeton, NJ: Ragged Sky Press.

Dening, Sarah. *The Everyday I Ching.* New York, NY: St. Martin's Griffin.

The ancient Chinese Book of Changes cultivates a daily experience of the dynamic nature of life and the inherent role of synchronicity. Taken together, these two books are excellent resources for training your heart and mind to relax with the larger order of the universe.

Gratitude

An excellent article on gratitude and the physiological impacts of this practice on the body: https://bit.ly/2GaDvEe

Within: Anchor to the Present

Heider, John. *The Tao of Leadership: Leadership Strategies for a New Age.* Atlanta, GA: Bantam Books.

An old yet always relevant resource for understanding how to lead from the inside out, letting the natural flow of life—the Tao—be your guide.

Tolle, Eckhart. *The Power of Now: A Guide to Spiritual Enlightenment.* Vancouver, BC, Canada: Namaste Publishing and Novato, CA: New World Library.

A tried-and-true classic offering guidance and direction on how to stay in the moment and reap the wisdom that comes when this capacity is built.

Below: Respect Creation

Kimmerer, Robin Wall. *Braiding Sweetgrass: Indigenous Wisdom, Scientific Knowledge, and the Teachings of Plants.* Minneapolis, MN: Milkweed Editions.

A beautiful and wise book filled with an awareness of the connection between living things and of the vibrant world we inhabit. It is written as a celebration of our reciprocal relationship with all creation.

East: Become Emotionally Agile

Johnson, Robert A. *Owning Your Own Shadow: Understanding the Dark Side of the Psyche.* New York, NY: Harper One.

Bly, Robert. *A Little Book on the Human Shadow*. New York, NY: HarperCollins.

These two books are short, poetic reads to open up the landscape of shadow and the importance of owning all aspects of ourselves.

Shadow Work

In-depth opportunities to work with and learn about the hidden gold in those aspects of yourself not fully owned. In addition to experiences and trainings, there is a wealth of valuable articles on this topic under the Features tab. Website: www.shadowwork.com

Sadness

An excellent article on grief and connection: https://bit.ly /2PhZC3e

South: Build Physical Resilience

Rath, Tom. *Are You Fully Charged? The 3 Keys to Energizing Your Work and Life*. US: Silicon Guild, an imprint of Missionday.

Simple, practical exercises, questions, and thoughts on organizing your work and life to ensure your "batteries" are fully charged.

Baumeister, Roy F. & Tierney, John. *Willpower: Rediscovering the Greatest Human Strength*. New York, NY: Penguin Books.

A thoughtful, well-researched read on why building clear, daily habits makes all the difference in being able to move toward a life well crafted.

West: Cultivate Mental Fluidity

Katie, Byron. *Loving What Is: Four Questions that Can Change Your Life.* New York, NY: Penguin Random House.
> A masterful guide to letting go of the stories you tell and releasing the emotions that accompany them.

Kagge, Erling. *Silence: In The Age of Noise.* New York, NY: Vintage Books.
> Thirty-one vignettes on the power, importance, and practice of silence.

LeClaire, Anne. *Listening Below the Noise: The Transformative Power of Silence.* New York, NY: HarperCollins.
> A personal experience of practicing silence twice a month for two decades, this book makes a profound case for how silence can transform your experience of the world.

Silent Together
> A monthly blog on the practice of silence and the opportunity to flex this muscle along with other around the globe during a monthly day of silence: https://www.silenttogether.com

North: Embrace Your Spiritual Destiny

Cecil, Barbara. *Coming Into Your Own: A Woman's Guide Through Life Transitions.* Ashland, OR: White Cloud Press.
> Candid stories of women around the world who have successfully navigated significant transitions, this book provides both the theory and the practices to find your way into the next stages of your life.

Baldwin, Christine. *Storycatcher: Making Sense of Our Lives Through the Power and Practice of Story.* Novato, CA: New World Library.

Filled with powerful and poignant stories of family, community, and self, this book opens the way to reconsider the stories you tell and learn how to write, speak, and recreate the personal narratives of your life.

Klaus Hempfling

Master teacher, coach, and mentor on the art and practice of tracking your destiny and living in accordance with your natural talents and aptitudes: https://www.hempfling.com

Acknowledgments

*W*hat a process it is to write a book! If I had known at the start the amount of work, rework, humility, and guts it takes, I suspect I would never have started. But I guess this is true for anything of value in this life. And like all things in life, it mainly took a community to get this book as an idea in my head onto the page and into print. For this community, I give deep thanks.

For the pioneering and steadfast souls who gently took the time to read the earliest drafts and then tell me I needed to throw them out and start over, I am totally indebted: Jody Simpson, my sister Sue, my father—who read multiple drafts and hung in there as I went from "Yes, seventy-two key concepts down to seven!"—and my tireless coach and agent, Jody Rein.

Key trusted friends gave their wisdom and support, reading drafts of either the manuscript or the book proposal: Christine Bader, Liz Davis, Aaron Frederick, Marian Goodman, Skip Griffin, and John Wipfler. Aaron sent me an unsolicited cover idea and photo which became the foundation for the beautiful cover design. Barbara Cecil stood steadily in the sidelines as I floated ideas and chapter notes into various programs we ran to see if the basic ideas were useful.

Stories abound, and I give thanks for all those who read their story and said, "Yes, indeed, go ahead, use it.": Cynthia Adams, Christine Bader, Catherine Braendel, Ross Curtis, Jane Frederick, Harv Forsgren, Gary Gillespie, Joan Brockway, Klaus Hempfling, Norbert Kemp, David Marsing, Jody Rein, Susann Shier, Jody Simpson, Michele Steckler, and Tamara Woodbury.

Much of my knowledge has come through the robust tussling, learning, thinking, and growing with dear colleagues and friends: Paul Alexander, Dorian Baroni, Kelvy Bird, Sarah Buie, Bradley Chenoweth, Skip Griffin, Glennifer Gillespie, Lise Hubbe, Bill Isaacs, Kate Isaacs, Cees Kramer, Margaret Krebs, David Miller, Cliff Penwell, Valentina Rodriguez, Kirsten Rowell, Sarah Rozenthuler, Elena Sadovnikova, Michele Steckler, and Marianne Williams.

I have had many teachers, guides, and mentors who either directly or indirectly kept me learning, questioning, curious, and humble. Three in particular I would honor whose wisdom has directly influenced the understandings represented in this book: Martin Cecil, David LaChapelle, and Klaus Hempfling. And my biggest teacher has been nature herself as friend, guardian, protector, disturber, and awakener of the beauty and power of all things large and small.

Reilly Dow, your incredible graphics bring the book to life! Co-agent Judy Klein, thank you for reaching out to She Writes Press. And Brooke Warner, Lauren Wise, Tabitha Lahr and all those behind the scenes, much gratitude for your care, patience, magical design skills and great work.

My sister Nancy, brother Al and life-long friends Maggie, Ann, Peg, Joan and John, I know you are always with me no matter what. To my husband Andrew, my deepest love and gratitude for your steady support, encouragement, and belief in me and my gifts. And finally, to Courtney, Lars, Gabe, and Silas: Continue to be your unique, talented and courageous selves and know the universe has your back every step of the way.

About the Graphics

Reilly Dow

*R*eilly is a listener, artist, and scribe. She grew up on Georgian Bay in Ontario, Canada, and is based in Mexico City. Working internationally in English and Spanish, she creates visuals that reflect both content and social process during conversations, meetings, and events. She holds a BA in early childhood education and an MA in interdisciplinary studies. Reilly's illustrations and artwork have been featured online as well as in books, academic publications, and presentations.

Photo © Daniel Cruz Rion

About the Author

*P*eri Chickering is an herbalist, coach, consultant, and leadership educator. Her early career as a mountaineer and wilderness guide took her traveling around the world. Out of these years she created wilderness-based leadership schools in South Africa and Bulgaria. Taking her leadership work from the outdoors inside, her clients now span private, governmental, and nonprofit sectors. Examples of the range of her clients include: Disney Theatrical, USDA Forest Service, World Bank, Stanford Woods Institute, University of Chicago, and Renaissance Reinsurance. She holds a master's in human development and a PhD in human and organizational systems. Situated in the small town of Hancock, NH, she, her husband, their cat, and two horses steward fifty-five acres of beautiful woodlands passed down from her grandmother.

Photo © Ann Foorman

NOTES

✦————————————✦

Prologue
"Recon: the Neacola Mountains," https://bit.ly/2UayAto

Chapter 1: Leadership Flow
Bud French passed away shortly before publication of this book. https://bit.ly/2XEv5h1

L'Amour, Louis. *The Lonesome Gods.* New York, NY: Bantam Books, 255.

"Killer Results without Killing Yourself," https://www.fastcompany.com/26491/killer-results-without-killing-yourself

Randall, Bob. The Land Owns Us. Global Oneness Project: https://www.globalonenessproject.org/library/films/land-owns-us

Chapter 3: How You Be Versus What You Do
Morgan, Peter, *Peter Morgan Serves the Queen, Again.* https://www.newyorker.com/culture/culture-desk/peter-morgan-serves-the-queen-again

"Leadership: What's love got to do with it?" https://www. oxfordleadership.com/wp-content/uploads/2016/08/ oxford-leadership-article-whats-love-got-to-do-with-it.pdf

Swimme, Brian, *The Hidden Heart of the Cosmos*. Maryknoll, NY: Orbis Books, 108.

Chapter 4: Above: Trust Life

Chinese Farmer parable, https://www.thebrightpath.com /blog/good-newsbad-news—who-knows

Zorba the Greek story, http://earthrenewal.org/bfly.htm

Chapter 5: Within: Anchor to the Present

"Bill Gates Took Solo 'Think Weeks,'" https://cnb.cx/2xL1uZK

"Meditation Brings Calm to CEOs," https://on.wsj.com/3aFPmre

L'Amour, Louis. *The Lonesome Gods*. New York, NY: Bantam Books, 62.

Rosa Parks biography, https://www.biography.com/activist /rosa-parks

McKeown, Greg, *Essentialism: The Disciplined Pursuit of Less*. New York: NY: Crown Publishing, 15.

Steindl-Rast, Brother David. *Gratefulness, the Heart of Prayer*. Ramsey, NJ: Paulist Press, 75.

Chapter 6: Below: Respect Creation

Blue Spruce, Duane & Thrasher, Tanya. *The Land has Memory: Indigenous Knowledge, Native Landscapes, and the National Museum of the American Indian*. Chapel Hill, NC: University of North Carolina Press & Smithsonian Institute, 43.

"Our Tribal Nature: Tribalism, Politics, and Evolution," https://bit.ly/31DdtW5

Conscious Capitalism, https://www.consciouscapitalism.org

Public Benefit Corporations, https://bit.ly/2BzCgj6

Berry, Wendell. *The Long-Legged House*. Berkeley, CA: Counterpoint, 220.

Chapter 7: Leadership Flow in Action

"The Role of Wind in a Tree's Life," https://awesci.com/the-role-of-wind-in-a-trees-life/

Chapter 8: East: Become Emotionally Agile

"What Google Learned From its Quest to Build the Perfect Team," https://www.nytimes.com/2016/02/28/magazine/what-google-learned-from-its-quest-to-build-the-perfect-team.html

Dakota Access Pipeline Protests, https://en.wikipedia.org/wiki/Dakota_Access_Pipeline_protests

"Veterans Came to North Dakota to Protest a Pipeline. But They also Found Healing and Forgiveness," https://www.latimes.com/nation/la-na-north-dakota-20161210-story.html

Chapter 9: South: Build Physical Resilience

Rath, Tom, *Are You Fully Charged? The Three Keys to Energizing Your Work and Life*. Jackson, TN: Silicon Guild, 121.

"Why Sleep is Essential for Health," https://www.medicalnewstoday.com/articles/325353

"New Research: How Employee Engagement Hits the Bottom Line," https://hbr.org/2012/11/creating-sustainable-employee.html

"Tsunami, 10 Years On: The Sea Nomads Who Survived the Devastation," https://www.theguardian.com/global-development/2014/dec/10/indian-ocean-tsunami-moken-sea-nomads-thailand

Observer Effect, https://simple.wikipedia.org/wiki/Observer_effect

"Biofield Science and Healing: History, Terminology, and Concepts," https://bit.ly/3eejDOW

Chapter 10: West: Cultivate Mental Fluidity

Silent Together, https://www.silenttogether.com

"Neuroscience Reveals 50-Year-Olds Can Have the Brains of 25-Year-Olds If They Do This 1 Thing," https://www.inc.com/melanie-curtin/neuroscience-shows-that-50-year-olds-can-have-brains-of-25-year-olds-if-they-do-this.html

L'Amour, Louis. *The Lonesome Gods.* New York, NY: Bantam Books, 371.

Ponca Chief White Eagle, https://www.okhistory.org/publications/enc/entry.php?entry=WH005

Berger, Warren. *A More Beautiful Question: The Power of Inquiry to Spark Breakthrough Ideas.* New York, NY: Bloomsbury.

Chapter 11: Embrace Your Spiritual Destiny

William Stafford, "The Way It Is" from Ask Me: 100 Essential Poems. Copyright © 1977, 2004 by William Stafford and the Estate of William Stafford. Reprinted with the permission of The Permissions Company, LLC on behalf of Graywolf Press, Minneapolis, Minnesota, graywolfpress.org.

O'Donohue, John, *Anam Cara: A Book of Celtic Wisdom.* New York, NY: Harper Collins, pg 83.

"Engaging Your Employees is Good, But Don't Stop There," https://hbr.org/2015/12/engaging-your-employees-is-good-but-dont-stop-there

"Abdul Satter Edhi, Known As 'Pakistan's Mother Teresa,' Dies at 88," https://www.npr.org/sections/parallels/2016/07/08/485279862/abdul-sattar-edhi-known-as-pakistans-mother-teresa-dies-at-88

Harvey, Andrew. https://theshiftnetwork.com/course/Sacred
　　Practices02/Salespage

Chapter 12: Return to We
Community Holistic Circle Healing, https://bit.ly/3d7MwNP
Become a Lake, https://www.awakin.org/read/view.php?tid=175
"Francisco De Roux, a Man of Faith Seeking Truth in Colom-
　　bia," https://colombiareports.com/francisco-de-roux-man
　　-faith-charge-finding-truth-colombia/
Council on the Uncertain Human Future, https://council
　　ontheuncertainhumanfuture.org/film/

SELECTED TITLES FROM SHE WRITES PRESS

She Writes Press is an independent publishing
company founded to serve women writers everywhere.
Visit us at www.shewritespress.com.

*The Way of the Mysterial Woman: Upgrading How You Live,
Love, and Lead* by Suzanne Anderson, MA and Susan Cannon,
PhD. $24.95, 978-1-63152-081-5. A revolutionary yet practical
road map for upgrading your life, work, and relationships that
reveals how your choice to transform is part of an astonishing
future trend.

*The Thriver's Edge: Seven Keys to Transform the Way You Live,
Love, and Lead* by Donna Stoneham. $16.95, 978-1-63152-
980-1. A "coach in a book" from master executive coach and
leadership expert Dr. Donna Stoneham, *The Thriver's Edge*
outlines a practical road map to breaking free of the barriers
keeping you from being everything you're capable of being.

Drop In: Lead with Deeper Presence and Courage by Sara
Harvey Yao. $14.95, 978-1-63152-161-4. A compelling expla-
nation about why being present is so challenging and how
leaders can access clarity, connection, and courage in the midst
of their chaotic lives, inside and outside of work.

*People Leadership: 30 Proven Strategies to Ensure Your Team's
Success* by Gina Folk. $24.95, 978-1-63152-915-3. Longtime
manager Gina Folk provides thirty effective ways for any individual managing or supervising others to reignite their team and
become a successful—and beloved—people leader.

*This Way Up: Seven Tools for Unleashing Your Creative Self
and Transforming Your Life* by Patti Clark. $16.95, 978-1-
63152-028-0. A story of healing for women who yearn to lead a
fuller life, accompanied by a workbook designed to help readers
work through personal challenges, discover new inspiration, and
harness their creative power.